New Perspectives on
Microsoft®
Access 97

BRIEF

Joseph J. Adamski
Grand Valley State University

Kathleen T. Finnegan

A Susan Solomon Book

COURSE
TECHNOLOGY

ONE MAIN STREET, CAMBRIDGE, MA 02142

an International Thomson Publishing company I(T)P®

Cambridge • Albany • Bonn • Boston • Cincinnati • London • Madrid • Melbourne • Mexico City
New York • Paris • San Francisco • Singapore • Tokyo • Toronto • Washington

New Perspectives on Microsoft® Access 97—Brief is published by Course Technology.

Associate Publisher	Mac Mendelsohn
Series Consulting Editor	Susan Solomon
Product Manager	Mark Reimold
Developmental Editor	Sasha Vodnik
Production Editor	Roxanne Alexander
Text and Cover Designer	Ella Hanna
Cover Illustrator	Douglas Goodman

© 1997 by Course Technology
A Division of International Thomson Publishing — I(T)P®

For more information contact:

Course Technology
One Main Street
Cambridge, MA 02142

International Thomson Publishing Europe
Berkshire House 168-173
High Holborn
London WCIV 7AA
England

Thomas Nelson Australia
102 Dodds Street
South Melbourne, 3205
Victoria, Australia

Nelson Canada
1120 Birchmount Road
Scarborough, Ontario
Canada M1K 5G4

International Thomson Editores
Campos Eliseos 385, Piso 7
Col. Polanco
11560 Mexico D.F. Mexico

International Thomson Publishing GmbH
Königswinterer Strasse 418
53227 Bonn
Germany

International Thomson Publishing Asia
211 Henderson Road
#05-10 Henderson Building
Singapore 0315

International Thomson Publishing Japan
Hirakawacho Kyowa Building, 3F
2-2-1 Hirakawacho
Chiyoda-ku, Tokyo 102
Japan

ISBN 0-7600-4552-6

Printed in the United States of America

10 9 8 7 6 5 4 3 2 1

What is the New Perspectives Series?

Course Technology's **New Perspectives Series** is an integrated system of instruction that combines text and technology products to teach computer concepts and micro-computer applications. Users consistently praise this series for innovative pedagogy, creativity, supportive and engaging style, accuracy, and use of interactive technology. The first New Perspectives text was published in January of 1993. Since then, the series has grown to more than 100 titles and has become the best-selling series on computer concepts and microcomputer applications. Others have imitated the New Perspectives features, design, and technologies, but none have replicated its quality and its ability to consistently anticipate and meet the needs of instructors and students.

How does this book I'm holding fit into the New Perspectives Series?

New Perspectives applications books are available in the following categories:

Brief books are typically about 160 pages long, contain two to four tutorials, and are intended to teach the basics of an application. The book you are holding is a Brief book.

Introductory books are typically about 300 pages long and consist of four to seven tutorials that go beyond the basics. These books often build out of the Brief editions by providing two or three additional tutorials.

Comprehensive books are typically about 600 pages long and consist of all of the tutorials in the Introductory books, plus four or five more tutorials covering higher-level topics. Comprehensive books also include two Windows tutorials, three or four Additional Cases, and a References section.

Advanced books cover topics similar to those in the Comprehensive books, but go into more depth. Advanced books present the most high-level coverage in the series.

Custom Books offer you two ways to customize a New Perspectives text to fit your course exactly: *CourseKits*™, two or more texts packaged together in a box, and *Custom Editions*®, your choice of books bound together. Custom Editions offer you unparalleled flexibility in designing your concepts and applications courses. You can build your own book by ordering a combination of titles bound together to cover only the topics you want. Your students save because they buy only the materials they need. There is no minimum order, and books are spiral bound. Both CourseKits and Custom Editions offer significant price discounts. Contact your Course Technology sales representative for more information.

New Perspectives Series Microcomputer Applications

■ Brief Titles or Modules	■ Introductory Titles or Modules	■ Intermediate Tutorials	■ Advanced Titles or Modules	☐ Other Modules
Brief	**Introductory**	**Comprehensive**	**Advanced**	**Custom Editions**
2 to 4 tutorials	6 or 7 tutorials, or Brief + 2 or 3 more tutorials	Introductory + 4 or 5 more tutorials. Includes Brief Windows tutorials, Additional Cases, and References section	Quick Review of basics + in-depth, high-level coverage	Choose from any of the above to build your own Custom Editions® or CourseKits™

How do the Windows 95 editions differ from the Windows 3.1 editions?

Sessions   We've divided the tutorials into sessions. Each session is designed to be completed in about 45 minutes to an hour (depending, of course, upon student needs and the speed of your lab equipment). With sessions, learning is broken up into more easily-assimilated portions. You can more accurately allocate time in your syllabus, and students can better manage the available lab time. Each session begins with a "session box," which quickly describes the skills students will learn in the session. Furthermore, each session is numbered, which makes it easier for you and your students to navigate and communicate about the tutorial. Look on page A 1.5 for the session box that opens Session 1.1.

Quick Checks   Each session concludes with meaningful, conceptual Quick Check questions that test students' understanding of what they learned in the session. Answers to all of the Quick Check questions in this book are provided on pages A 4.35 through A 4.36.

New Design   We have retained the best of the old design to help students differentiate between what they are to *do* and what they are to *read*. The steps are clearly identified by their shaded background and numbered steps. Furthermore, this new design presents steps and screen shots in a larger, easier to read format. Some good examples of our new design are pages A 1.14 and A 1.15.

What features are retained in the Windows 95 editions of the New Perspectives Series?

"Read This Before You Begin" Page   This page is consistent with Course Technology's unequaled commitment to helping instructors introduce technology into the classroom. Technical considerations and assumptions about software are listed to help instructors save time and eliminate unnecessary aggravation. See page A 1.2 for the "Read This Before You Begin" page in this book.

Tutorial Case   Each tutorial begins with a problem presented in a case that is meaningful to students. The problem turns the task of learning how to use an application into a problem-solving process. The problems increase in complexity with each tutorial. These cases touch on multicultural, international, and ethical issues—so important to today's business curriculum. See page A 1.3 for the case that begins Tutorial 1.

1.
2.
3.

Step-by-Step Methodology   This unique Course Technology methodology keeps students on track. They enter data, click buttons, or press keys always within the context of solving the problem posed in the tutorial case. The text constantly guides students, letting them know where they are in the course of solving the problem. In addition, the numerous screen shots include labels that direct students' attention to what they should look at on the screen. On almost every page in this book, you can find an example of how steps, screen shots, and labels work together.

TROUBLE?

TROUBLE? Paragraphs   These paragraphs anticipate the mistakes or problems that students are likely to have and help them recover and continue with the tutorial. By putting these paragraphs in the book, rather than in the Instructor's Manual, we facilitate independent learning and free the instructor to focus on substantive conceptual issues rather than on common procedural errors. Two representative examples of TROUBLE? paragraphs are on pages A 1.7 and A 1.10.

Reference Windows   Reference Windows appear throughout the text. They are succinct summaries of the most important tasks covered in the tutorials. Reference Windows are specially designed and written so students can refer to them when doing the Tutorial Assignments and Case Problems, and after completing the course. Page A 1.18 contains the Reference Window for Using the Office Assistant.

Task Reference The Task Reference contains a summary of how to perform common tasks using the most efficient method, as well as references to pages where the task is discussed in more detail. It appears as a table at the end of the book.

Tutorial Assignments, Case Problems, and Lab Assignments Each tutorial concludes with Tutorial Assignments, which provide students with additional hands-on practice of the skills they learned in the tutorial. See page A 1.23 for examples of Tutorial Assignments. The Tutorial Assignments are followed by four Case Problems that have approximately the same scope as the tutorial case. See page A 1.24 for examples of Case Problems. Finally, if a Course Lab accompanies a tutorial, Lab Assignments are included after the Case Problems. See page A 1.27 for examples of Lab Assignments.

Exploration Exercises The Windows environment allows students to learn by exploring and discovering what they can do. Exploration Exercises can be Tutorial Assignments or Case Problems that challenge students, encourage them to explore the capabilities of the program they are using, and extend their knowledge using the Help facility and other reference materials. Page A 1.23 contains Exploration Exercises for Tutorial 1.

What supplements are available with this textbook?

Course Labs: Now, Concepts Come to Life Computer skills and concepts come to life with the New Perspectives Course Labs—highly-interactive tutorials that combine illustrations, animations, digital images, and simulations. The Labs guide students step-by-step, present them with Quick Check questions, let them explore on their own, test their comprehension, and provide printed feedback. Lab icons at the beginning of the tutorial and in the tutorial margins indicate when a topic has a corresponding Lab. Lab Assignments are included at the end of each relevant tutorial. The Lab available with this book and the tutorial in which it appears is:

TUTORIAL 1

Databases

Course Test Manager: Testing and Practice at the Computer or on Paper Course Test Manager is cutting-edge, Windows-based testing software that helps instructors design and administer practice tests and actual examinations. This full-featured program allows students to randomly generate practice tests that provide immediate on-screen feedback and detailed study guides. Instructors can also use Course Test Manager to produce printed tests. Course Test Manager can automatically grade the tests students take at the computer and can generate statistical information on individual as well as group performance.

Online Companions: Dedicated to Keeping You and Your Students Up-To-Date When you use a New Perspectives product, you can access Course Technology's faculty sites and student sites on the World Wide Web. You can browse the password-protected Faculty Online Companions to obtain online Instructor's Manuals, Solution Files, Student Files, and more. Please see your Instructor's Manual or call your Course Technology customer service representative for more information. Student and Faculty Online Companions are accessible by clicking the appropriate links on Course Technology's home page at **http://www.course.com**.

Instructor's Manual New Perspectives Series Instructor's Manuals contain instructor's notes and printed solutions for each tutorial. Instructor's notes provide tutorial overviews and outlines, technical notes, lecture notes, and extra case problems. Printed solutions include solutions to Tutorial Assignments, Case Problems, and Lab Assignments.

Student Files Student Files contain all of the data that students will use to complete the tutorials, Tutorial Assignments, and Case Problems. A Readme file includes technical tips for lab management. See the inside covers of this book and the "Read This Before You Begin" page before Tutorial 1 for more information on Student Files.

Internet Assignments The Instructor's Manual that accompanies this book includes additional assignments that integrate the World Wide Web with the database skills students learn in the tutorials. To complete these assignments, students will need to search the Web and follow the links from the New Perspectives on Microsoft Office 97 home page. The Office 97 home page is accessible through the Student Online Companions link found on the Course Technology home page at **http://www.course.com.** Please refer to the Instructor's Manual for more information.

Solution Files Solution Files contain every file students are asked to create or modify in the tutorials, Tutorial Assignments, and Case Problems.

The following supplements are included in the Instructor's Resource Kit that accompanies this textbook:

- Instructor's Manual
- Solution Files
- Student Files
- Databases Course Lab
- Course Test Manager Release 1.1 Test Bank
- Course Test Manager Release 1.1 Engine

Some of the supplements listed above are also available over the World Wide Web through Course Technology's password-protected Faculty Online Companions. Please see your Instructor's Manual or call your Course Technology customer service representative for more information.

Acknowledgments

I would like to thank the dedicated and enthusiastic Course Technology staff, including Joe Dougherty, Mac Mendelsohn, Susan Solomon, and Mark Reimold. Thanks as well to all the Production staff, including everyone from GEX who worked hard to produce this book. And a special thanks to Kathy Finnegan for her talents, verve, and long hours of dedicated work.

Joseph J. Adamski

I would like to thank the following reviewers for their excellent feedback and helpful suggestions: Cynthia J. Kachik, Jean Smelewicz of Quinsigamond Community College, and Patricia A. Smith, Ph.D., of Temple Junior College. Also, my thanks to all the Course Technology staff, including Mac Mendelsohn, Mark Reimold, Rachel Crapser, and Kristen Duerr for enabling me to complete this book and for their support; Roxanne Alexander for her outstanding management of the production process; Jane Pedicini for her superior copy editing skills; Christine Smith, for her attention to detail; Alexandra Nickerson for producing the index; and Greg Bigelow, and Brian McCooey, for ensuring the accuracy of the text. Thanks, too, to everyone at GEX for their efforts in the composition of this book. Special thanks to Sasha Vodnik for his insightful contributions in developing and testing this text, and to Joe Adamski for his invaluable guidance and encouragement throughout this project.

Finally, thanks to Joe, Connor, and Devon for their support and for interrupting me just enough so that I remembered what the outside of my office looked like.

Kathleen T. Finnegan

Table of **Contents**

Microsoft®
Access 97

LEVEL I

TUTORIALS

Read This **Before You Begin**

STUDENT DISKS

To complete Access 97 Tutorials 1-4, you need three Student Disks. Your instructor will either provide you with the Student Disks or ask you to make your own.

If you are supposed to make your own Student Disks, you will need three blank, formatted, high-density disks. You will need to copy a set of folders from a file server or standalone computer onto your disks. Your instructor will tell you which computer, drive letter, and folders contain the files you need. The following table shows you which folders go on each of your disks, so that you will have enough disk space to complete all the tutorials, Tutorial Assignments, and Case Problems:

Student Disk	Write this on the disk label	Put these folders on the disk
1	Student Disk 1: Access 97 Tutorials 1-4 Tutorials and Tutorial Assignments	Tutorial and TAssign from Disk 1 folder
2	Student Disk 2: Access 97 Case Problems 1 and 2	Cases from Disk 2 folder
3	Student Disk 3: Access 97 Case Problems 3 and 4	Cases from Disk 3 folder

When you begin each tutorial, be sure you are using the correct Student Disk. See the inside front or inside back cover of this book for more information on Student Disk files, or ask your instructor or technical support person for assistance.

COURSE LAB

Tutorial 1 features an interactive Course Lab to help you understand database concepts. There are Lab Assignments at the end of the tutorial that relate to this Lab. To start the Lab, click the Start button on the Windows 95 taskbar, point to Programs, point to Course Labs, point to New Perspectives Applications, and click Databases.

USING YOUR OWN COMPUTER

If you are going to work through this book using your own computer, you need:

■ **Computer System** Microsoft Windows 95 or Microsoft Windows NT Workstation 4.0 and Microsoft Access 97 must be installed on your computer. This book assumes a typical installation of Microsoft Access 97.

■ **Student Disks** Ask your instructor or lab manager for details on how to get the Student Disks. You will not be able to complete the tutorials or end-of-tutorial assignments in this book using your own computer until you have the Student Disks. The Student Files may also be obtained electronically over the Internet. See the inside front or inside back cover of this book for more details.

■ **Course Lab** See your instructor or technical support person to obtain the Course Lab software for use on your own computer.

To complete Access 97 Tutorials 1-4, your students must use a set of files on three Student Disks. These files are included in the Instructor's Resource Kit, and they may also be obtained electronically over the Internet. See the inside front or inside back cover of this book for more details. Follow the instructions in the Readme file to copy the files to your server or standalone computer. You can view the Readme file using WordPad. Once the files are copied, you can make Student Disks for the students yourself, or you can tell students where to find the files so they can make their own Student Disks.

COURSE LAB SOFTWARE

The Course Lab software is distributed on a CD-ROM included in the Instructor's Resource Kit. To install the Course Lab software, follow the setup instructions in the Readme file on the CD-ROM. Refer also to the Readme file for essential technical notes related to running the Lab in a multi-user environment. Once you have installed the Course Lab software, your students can start the Lab from the Windows 95 desktop by following the instructions in the Course Lab section above.

COURSE TECHNOLOGY STUDENT FILES AND LAB SOFTWARE

You are granted a license to copy the Student Files and Lab software to any computer or computer network used by students who have purchased this book.

TUTORIAL 1

Introduction to Microsoft Access 97

Viewing and Working with a Table Containing Customer Data

In this tutorial you will:

- Define the terms field, record, table, relational database, primary key, and foreign key

- Start and exit Access

- Open an existing database

- Identify the components of the Access and Database windows

- Open, navigate, and print a table

- Create, run, and print a query

- Create and print a form

- Use the Access Help system

- Create, preview, and print a report

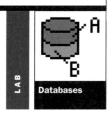

LAB

Databases

Valle Coffee

CASE

Ten years ago Leonard Valle became the president of Algoman Imports, a small distributor of inexpensive coffee beans to supermarkets in western Michigan. At that time the company's growth had leveled off, so during his first three years Leonard took several dramatic, risky steps in an attempt to increase sales and profits. First, he changed the inexpensive coffee bean varieties that Algoman Imports had been distributing to a selection of gourmet varieties from Central and South America, Africa, and several island nations. Second, he purchased facilities and equipment so that the company could roast, grind, flavor, and package the coffee beans instead of buying them already roasted and packaged whole. Because the company could now control the quality of the finest gourmet coffees, Leonard stopped distributing to supermarkets and shifted sales to restaurants and offices throughout the area.

Within two years, company sales and profits soared; consequently, Leonard took over ownership of the company. He changed the company name to Valle Coffee, continued expanding into other markets and geographic areas (specifically, Ohio and Indiana), and expanded the company's line of coffee flavors and blends.

Part of Valle Coffee's success can be credited to its use of computers in all aspects of its business, including financial management, inventory control, shipping, receiving, production, and sales. Several months ago the company upgraded to Microsoft Windows 95 and **Microsoft Access 97** (or simply **Access**), a computer program used to enter, maintain, and retrieve related data in a format known as a database. Barbara Hennessey, office manager at Valle Coffee, and her staff use Access to maintain company data such as customer orders and billing, coffee supplier orders and payments, and advertising placements and payments. Barbara recently created a database named Restaurant to track the company's restaurant customers, their orders, and related data such as the products they order. She asks for your help in completing and maintaining this database.

Using the Tutorials Effectively

These tutorials are designed to be used at a computer. Each tutorial is divided into sessions. Watch for the session headings, such as "Session 1.1" and "Session 1.2." Each session is designed to be completed in about 45 minutes, but take as much time as you need. When you've completed a session, it's a good idea to exit the program and take a break. You can exit Microsoft Access by clicking the Close button in the top-right corner of the program window.

Before you begin, read the following questions and answers. They are designed to help you use the tutorials effectively.

Where do I start?

Each tutorial begins with a case, which sets the scene for the tutorial and gives you background information to help you understand what you will be doing in the tutorial. Read the case before you go to the lab. In the lab, begin with the first session of the tutorial.

How do I know what to do on the computer?

Each session contains steps that you will perform on the computer to learn how to use Microsoft Access. The steps are numbered and are set against a colored background. Read the text that introduces each series of steps, and read each step carefully and completely before you try it.

How do I know if I did the step correctly?

As you work, compare your computer screen with the corresponding figure in the tutorial. Don't worry if your screen display is somewhat different from the figure. The important parts of the screen display are labeled in each figure. Check to make sure these parts are on your screen.

What if I make a mistake?

Don't worry about making mistakes—they are part of the learning process. Paragraphs labeled **"TROUBLE?"** identify common problems and explain how to get back on track. Follow the steps in a **"TROUBLE?"** paragraph *only* if you are having the problem described. If you run into other problems, carefully consider the current state of your system, the position of the pointer, and any messages on the screen.

How do I use the Reference Windows?

Reference Windows summarize the procedures you learn in the tutorial steps. Do not complete the actions in the Reference Windows when you are working through the tutorial. Instead, refer to the Reference Windows while you are working on the assignments at the end of the tutorial.

How can I test my understanding of the material I learned in the tutorial?

At the end of each session, you can answer the Quick Check questions. If necessary, refer to the Answers to Quick Check Questions to check your work.

After you have completed the entire tutorial, you should complete the Tutorial Assignments and Case Problems. These exercises are carefully structured so you will review what you have learned and then apply your knowledge to new situations.

What if I can't remember how to do something?

You should refer to the Task Reference at the end of the book; it summarizes how to accomplish commonly performed tasks.

What is the Databases Course Lab, and how should I use it?

This interactive Lab helps you review database concepts and practice skills that you learn in Tutorial 1. The Lab Assignments section at the end of Tutorial 1 includes instructions for using the Lab.

Now that you've seen how to use the tutorials effectively, you are ready to begin.

SESSION

1.1

In this session you will define key database terms and concepts, start Access and open an existing database, identify components of the Access and Database windows, open and navigate a table, print a table, and exit Access.

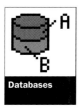

Databases

Introduction to Database Concepts

Before you begin working on Barbara's database and using Access, you need to understand a few key terms and concepts associated with databases.

Organizing Data

Data is a valuable resource to any business. At Valle Coffee, for example, important data includes customers' names and addresses, and order dates and amounts. Organizing, storing, maintaining, retrieving, and sorting this type of data are critical activities that enable a business to find and use information effectively. Before storing data on a computer, however, you first must organize the data.

Your first step in organizing data is to identify the individual fields. A **field** is a single characteristic or attribute of a person, place, object, event, or idea. For example, some of the many fields that Valle Coffee tracks are customer number, customer name, customer address, customer phone number, order number, billing date, and invoice amount.

Next, you group related fields together into tables. A **table** is a collection of fields that describe a person, place, object, event, or idea. Figure 1-1 shows an example of a Customer table consisting of four fields: Customer Number, Customer Name, Customer Address, and Phone Number.

Figure 1-1 ◀
Data
organization for
a table of
customers

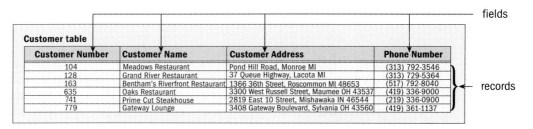

fields

records

The specific value, or content, of a field is called the **field value**. In Figure 1-1, the first set of field values for Customer Number, Customer Name, Customer Address, and Phone Number are, respectively, 104; Meadows Restaurant; Pond Hill Road, Monroe MI 48161; and (313) 792-3546. This set of field values is called a **record**. In the Customer table, the data for each customer is stored as a separate record. Six records are shown in Figure 1-1; each row of field values is a record.

Databases and Relationships

A collection of related tables is called a **database**, or **relational database**. Valle Coffee's Restaurant database will contain two related tables: the Customer table, which Barbara has already created, and the Order table, which you will create in Tutorial 2. Sometimes you might want information about customers and the orders they placed. To obtain this information you must have a way to connect records in the Customer table to records in the Order table. You connect the records in the separate tables through a **common field** that appears in both tables. In the sample database shown in Figure 1-2, each record in the Customer table has a field named Customer Number, which is also a field in the Order table. For example, Oaks Restaurant is the fourth customer in the Customer table and has a Customer Number of 635. This same Customer Number field value, 635, appears in three records in the Order table. Therefore, Oaks Restaurant is the customer that placed these three orders.

Figure 1-2 ◀
Database
relationship
between tables
for customers
and orders

primary keys

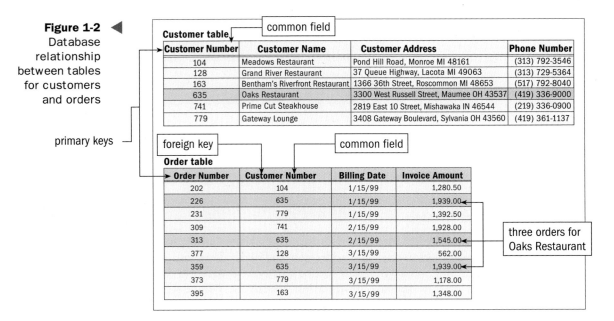

Each Customer Number in the Customer table must be unique, so that you can distinguish one customer from another and identify the customer's specific orders in the Order table. The Customer Number field is referred to as the primary key of the Customer table. A **primary key** is a field, or a collection of fields, whose values uniquely identify each record in a table. In the Order table, Order Number is the primary key.

When you include the primary key from one table as a field in a second table to form a relationship between the two tables, it is called a **foreign key** in the second table, as shown in Figure 1-2. For example, Customer Number is the primary key in the Customer table and a foreign key in the Order table. Although the primary key Customer Number has unique values in the Customer table, the same field as a foreign key in the Order table does not have unique values. The Customer Number value 635, for example, appears three times in the Order table, because the Oaks Restaurant placed three orders. Each foreign key value, however, must match one of the field values for the primary key in the other table. In the example in Figure 1-2, each Customer Number value in the Order table must match a Customer Number value in the Customer table. The two tables are related, enabling users to tie together the facts about customers with the facts about orders.

Relational Database Management Systems

To manage its databases, a company purchases a database management system. A **database management system** (**DBMS**) is a software program that lets you create databases and then manipulate data in the databases. Most of today's database management systems, including Access, are called relational database management systems. In a **relational database management system**, data is organized as a collection of tables. As stated earlier, a relationship between two tables in a relational DBMS is formed through a common field.

A relational DBMS controls the storage of databases on disk by carrying out data creation and manipulation requests. Specifically, a relational DBMS provides the following functions, which are illustrated in Figure 1-3:

■ It allows you to create database structures containing fields, tables, and table relationships.

■ It lets you easily add new records, change field values in existing records, and delete records.

■ It contains a built-in query language, which lets you obtain immediate answers to the questions you ask about your data.

- It contains a built-in report generator, which lets you produce professional-looking, formatted reports from your data.

- It provides protection of databases through security, control, and recovery facilities.

Figure 1-3 ◀
A relational
database
management
system

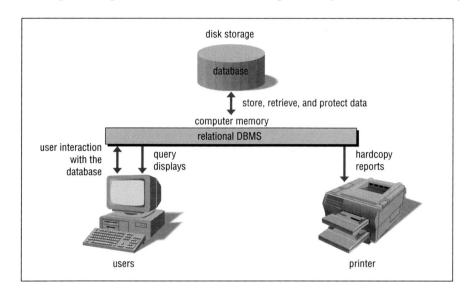

A company like Valle Coffee benefits from a relational DBMS because it allows several users working in different departments to share the same data. More than one user can enter data into a database, and more than one user can retrieve and analyze data that was entered by others. For example, Valle Coffee will keep only one copy of the Customer table, and all employees will be able to use it to meet their specific needs for customer information.

Finally, unlike other software programs, such as spreadsheets, a DBMS can handle massive amounts of data and can easily form relationships among multiple tables. Each Access database, for example, can be up to 1 gigabyte in size and can contain up to 32,768 objects (tables, queries, and so on).

Now that you've learned some database terms and concepts, you're ready to start Access and open the Restaurant database.

Starting Access

You start Access in the same way that you start other Windows 95 programs—using the Start button on the taskbar.

To start Access:

1. Make sure Windows 95 is running on your computer and the Windows 95 desktop appears on your screen.

   TROUBLE? If you're running Windows NT Workstation 4.0 (or a later version) on your computer or network, don't worry. Although the figures in this book were created while running Windows 95, Windows NT 4.0 and Windows 95 share the same interface, and Access 97 runs equally well under either operating system.

2. Click the **Start** button on the taskbar to display the Start menu, and then point to **Programs** to display the Programs menu.

3. Point to **Microsoft Access** on the Programs menu. See Figure 1-4.

Figure 1-4 ◀
Starting
Microsoft
Access

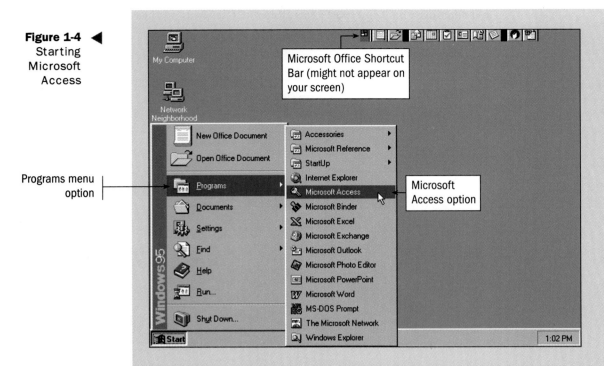

Programs menu
option

TROUBLE? If you don't see the Microsoft Access option on the Programs menu, ask your instructor or technical support person for help.

TROUBLE? The Office Shortcut Bar, which appears along the top of the desktop in Figure 1-4, might look different on your screen or it might not appear at all, depending on how your system is set up. The steps in these tutorials do not require that you use the Office Shortcut Bar; therefore, the remaining figures do not display the Office Shortcut Bar.

4. Click **Microsoft Access** to start Access. After a short pause, the Access copyright information appears in a message box and remains on the screen until the Access window is displayed. See Figure 1-5.

Figure 1-5 ◀
The Microsoft
Access window

toolbar

initial dialog box

status bar

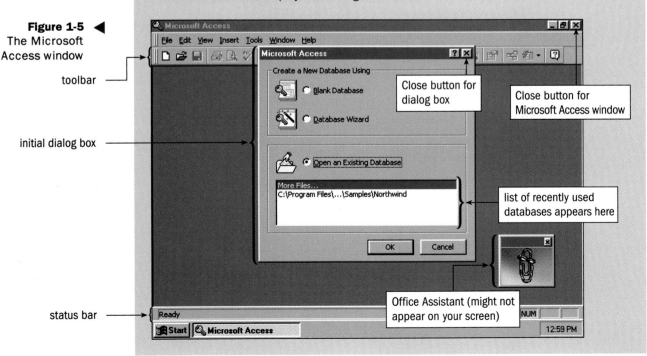

TROUBLE? Depending on how your system is set up, the Office Assistant (see Figure 1-5) might open when you start Access. For now, click the Close button ☒ on the Office Assistant window to close it; you'll learn more about this feature later in this tutorial. If you've started Access immediately after installing it, you'll need to click the Start Using Microsoft Access option, which the Office Assistant displays, before closing the Office Assistant window.

When you start Access, the Access window contains a dialog box that allows you to create a new database or open an existing database. You can choose either the Blank Database option to create a new database on your own, or you can choose the Database Wizard option and let the wizard guide you through the steps for creating a database. In this case, you need to open an existing database.

Opening an Existing Database

To open an existing database, you can select the name of a database in the list of recently opened databases (if the list appears), or you can choose the More Files option to open a database not listed. You need to open an existing database—the Restaurant database on your Student Disk.

To open the Restaurant database:

1. Make sure you have created your copy of the Access Student Disk, and then place your Student Disk in the appropriate disk drive.

   TROUBLE? If you don't have a Student Disk, you need to get one before you can proceed. Your instructor will either give you one or ask you to make your own. (See your instructor for information.) In either case, be sure you have made a copy of your Student Disk before you begin; in this way, the original Student Disk files will be available on the copied disk in case you need to start over because of an error or problem.

2. In the Microsoft Access dialog box, make sure the **Open an Existing Database** option button is selected. Also, if your dialog box contains a list of files, make sure the **More Files** option is selected.

3. Click the **OK** button to display the Open dialog box. See Figure 1-6.

Figure 1-6 ◄
Open dialog box

Look in list box

list of folders and database files in current folder

click to display the list of available drives and folders

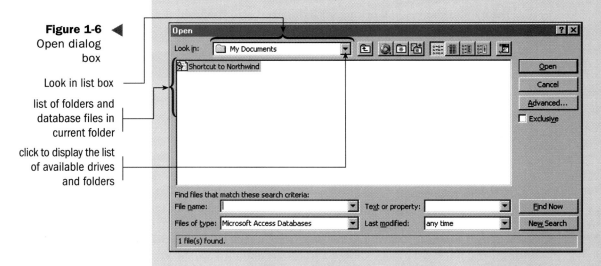

TROUBLE? The list of folders and files on your screen might be different from the list in Figure 1-6.

4. Click the **Look in** list arrow, and then click the drive that contains your Student Disk.

5. Click **Tutorial** in the list box (if necessary), and then click the **Open** button to display a list of the files in the Tutorial folder.

6. Click **Restaurant** in the list box, and then click the **Open** button. The Restaurant database is displayed in the Access window. See Figure 1-7.

Figure 1-7 ◀
Access and
Database
windows

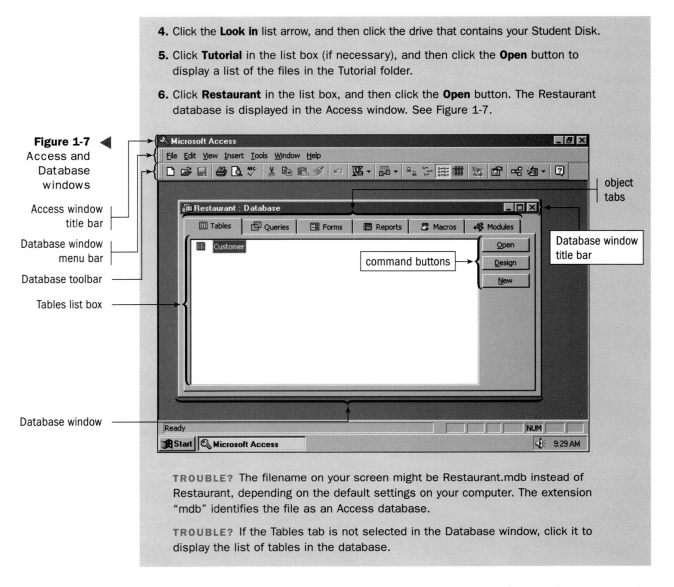

Access window
title bar

Database window
menu bar

Database toolbar

Tables list box

object
tabs

Database window
title bar

command buttons

Database window

TROUBLE? The filename on your screen might be Restaurant.mdb instead of Restaurant, depending on the default settings on your computer. The extension "mdb" identifies the file as an Access database.

TROUBLE? If the Tables tab is not selected in the Database window, click it to display the list of tables in the database.

Before you can begin working with the database, you need to become familiar with the components of the Access and Database windows.

The Access and Database Windows

The **Access window** is the program window that appears when you start the program. The **Database window** appears when you open a database; this window is the main control center for working with an open Access database. Except for the Access window title bar, all screen components now on your screen are associated with the Database window (see Figure 1-7). Most of these screen components—including the title bars, window sizing buttons, menu bar, toolbar, and status bar—are the same as the components in other Windows 95 programs.

The Database window contains six object tabs. Each **object tab** controls one of the six major object groups, such as tables, in an Access database. (In addition to tables, you'll work with queries, forms, and reports later in this book; macros and modules are used for more complex database design and programming and, therefore, are outside the scope of this text.)

Barbara has already created the Customer table in the Restaurant database. She suggests that you open the Customer table and view its contents.

Opening an Access Table

As noted earlier, tables contain all the data in a database. Tables are the fundamental objects for your work in Access. To view, add, change, or delete data in a table, you first must open the table. You can open any Access object by using the Open button in the Database window.

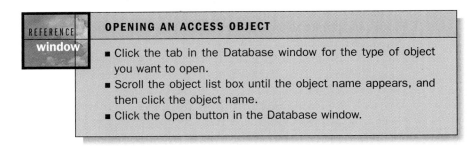

REFERENCE window

OPENING AN ACCESS OBJECT

- Click the tab in the Database window for the type of object you want to open.
- Scroll the object list box until the object name appears, and then click the object name.
- Click the Open button in the Database window.

You need to open the Customer table, which is the only table currently in the Restaurant database.

To open the Customer table:

1. If the Customer table is not highlighted, click **Customer** to select it.

2. Click the **Open** button in the Database window. The Customer table opens in Datasheet view on top of the Database and Access windows. See Figure 1-8.

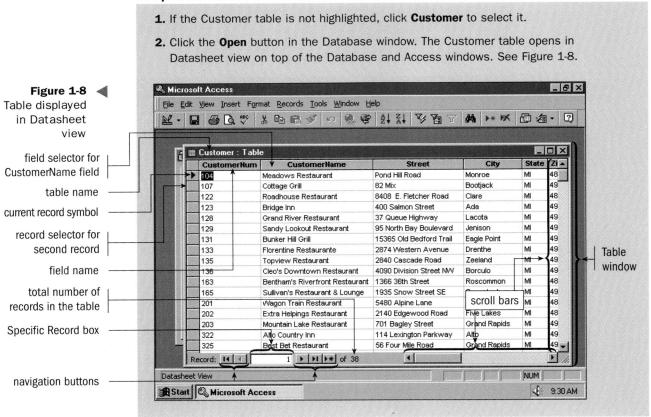

Figure 1-8
Table displayed in Datasheet view

field selector for CustomerName field

table name

current record symbol

record selector for second record

field name

total number of records in the table

Specific Record box

navigation buttons

Table window

scroll bars

Datasheet view shows a table's contents as a **datasheet** in rows and columns, similar to a table or spreadsheet. Each row is a separate record in the table, and each column contains the field values for one field in the table. Each column is headed by a field name inside a field selector, and each row has a record selector to its left. Clicking a **field selector** or a **record selector** selects that entire column or row (respectively), which you can then manipulate. A field selector is also called a **column selector**, and a record selector is also called a **row selector**.

Navigating an Access Datasheet

When you first open a datasheet, Access selects the first field value in the first record. Notice that this field value is highlighted and that a darkened triangle symbol, called the current record symbol, appears in the record selector to the left of the first record. The **current record symbol** identifies the currently selected record. Clicking a record selector or field value in another row moves the current record symbol to that row. You can also move the pointer over the data on the screen and click one of the field values to position the insertion point.

The Customer table currently has nine fields and 38 records. To view fields or records not currently visible in the datasheet, you can use the horizontal and vertical scroll bars shown in Figure 1-8 to navigate through the data. The **navigation buttons**, also shown in Figure 1-8, provide another way to move vertically through the records. Figure 1-9 shows which record becomes the current record when you click each navigation button. The **Specific Record box**, which appears between the two sets of navigation buttons, displays the current record number; and the total number of records in the table appears to the right of the navigation buttons.

Figure 1-9 ◀
Navigation
buttons

Navigation Button	Record Selected	Navigation Button	Record Selected
⏮	First Record	⏭	Last Record
◀	Previous Record	▶*	New Record
▶	Next Record		

Barbara suggests that you use the various navigation techniques to move through the Customer table and become familiar with its contents.

To navigate the Customer datasheet:

1. Click the right arrow button in the horizontal scroll bar a few times to scroll to the right and view the remaining fields in the Customer table.

2. Drag the scroll box in the horizontal scroll bar back to the left to return to the previous display of the datasheet.

3. Click the **Next Record** navigation button ▶. The second record is now the current record, as indicated by the current record symbol in the second record selector. Also, notice that the second record's value for the CustomerNum field is highlighted, and "2" (for record number 2) appears in the Specific Record box.

4. Click the **Last Record** navigation button ⏭. The last record in the table, record 38, is now the current record.

5. Click the **Previous Record** navigation button ◀. Record 37 is now the current record.

6. Click the **First Record** navigation button ⏮. The first record is now the current record.

Next, Barbara asks you to print the Customer table so that you can refer to it as you continue working with the Restaurant database.

Printing a Table

In Access you can print a table using either the Print command on the File menu or the Print button on the toolbar. The Print command displays a dialog box in which you can specify print settings. The Print button prints the table using the current settings. You'll use the Print button to print the Customer table.

To print the Customer table:

1. Click the **Print** button 🖨 on the Table Datasheet toolbar. Because all of the fields can't fit across one page, the table prints on two pages. You'll learn how to specify different print settings in later tutorials.

Now that you've viewed and printed the Customer table, you can exit Access.

Exiting Access

To exit Access, you simply click the Close button on the Access window title bar. When exiting, Access closes any open tables and the open database before closing the program.

To exit Access:

1. Click the **Close** button ⊠ on the Access window title bar. The Customer table and the Restaurant database close, Access closes, and you return to the Windows 95 desktop.

Quick Check

1. A(n) _____ is a single characteristic of a person, place, object, event, or idea.

2. You connect the records in two separate tables through a(n) _____ that appears in both tables.

3. The _____, whose values uniquely identify each record in a table, is called a _____ when it is placed in a second table to form a relationship between the two tables.

4. In a table, the rows are called _____ and the columns are called _____.

5. The _____ identifies the selected record in an Access table.

6. Describe the two methods for navigating through a table.

Now that you've become familiar with Access and the Resturant database, you're ready to work with the data stored in the database.

SESSION 1.2	*In this session you will create and print a query; create and print a form; use the Help system; and create, preview, and print a report.*

Kim Carpenter, the director of marketing at Valle Coffee, wants a list of all restaurant customers so that her staff can call customers to check on their satisfaction with Valle

Coffee's services and products. She doesn't want the list to include all the fields in the Customer table (such as Street and ZipCode). To produce this list for Kim, you need to create a query using the Customer table.

Creating and Printing a Query

A **query** is a question you ask about the data stored in a database. In response to a query, Access displays the specific records and fields that answer your question. When you create a query, you tell Access which fields you need and what criteria Access should use to select the records. Access then displays only the information you want, so you don't have to scan through the entire database for the information.

You can design your own queries or use an Access **Query Wizard**, which guides you through the steps to create a query. The Simple Query Wizard allows you to select records and fields quickly, and is an appropriate choice for producing the customer list Kim wants.

To start the Simple Query Wizard:

1. Insert your Student Disk in the appropriate disk drive.

2. Start Access, make sure the **Open an Existing Database** option button is selected and the **More Files** option is selected, and then click the **OK** button to display the Open dialog box.

3. Click the **Look in** list arrow, click the drive that contains your Student Disk, click **Tutorial** in the list box, and then click the **Open** button to display the list of files in the Tutorial folder.

4. Click **Restaurant** in the list box, and then click the **Open** button.

5. Click the **Queries** tab in the Database window to display the Queries list. The Queries list box is empty because you haven't defined any queries yet.

6. Click the **New** button to open the New Query dialog box.

7. Click **Simple Query Wizard** and then click the **OK** button. The first Simple Query Wizard dialog box opens. See Figure 1-10.

Figure 1-10 ◀
First Simple
Query Wizard
dialog box

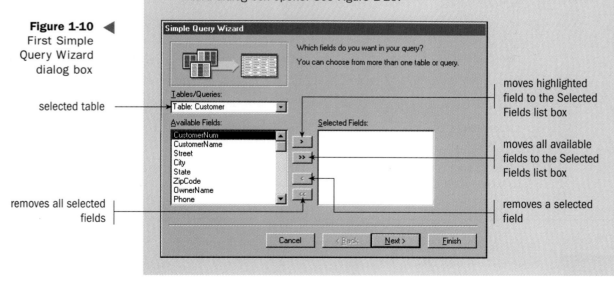

selected table

removes all selected
fields

Because Customer is the only object currently in the Restaurant database, it is listed in the Tables/Queries box. You could click the Tables/Queries list arrow to choose another table or a query on which to base the query you're creating. The Available Fields box lists the fields in the selected table (in this case, Customer). You need to select fields from this list to include them in the query. To select fields one at a time, click a field and then click the ▸ button. The selected field moves from the Available Fields list box on the left to the Selected Fields list box on the right. To select all the fields, click the ⟦ » ⟧ button. If you change your mind or make a mistake, you can remove a field by clicking it in the Selected Fields list box and then clicking the ⟦ ‹ ⟧ button. To remove all selected fields, click the ⟦ « ⟧ button.

Each wizard dialog box contains buttons on the bottom that allow you to move to the previous dialog box (Back button), the next dialog box (Next button), or to cancel the creation process (Cancel button) and return to the Database window. You can also finish creating the object (Finish button) and accept the wizard's defaults for the remaining options.

Kim wants her list to include data from only the following fields: CustomerNum, CustomerName, City, State, OwnerName, and Phone. You need to select these fields to be included in the query.

To create the query using the Simple Query Wizard:

1. Click **CustomerNum** in the Available Fields list box (if necessary), and then click the ⟦ › ⟧ button. The CustomerNum field moves to the Selected Fields list box.

2. Repeat Step 1 for the fields **CustomerName**, **City**, **State**, **OwnerName**, and **Phone**, and then click the **Next** button. The second, and final, Simple Query Wizard dialog box opens and asks you to choose a name for your query. This name will appear in the Queries list in the Database window. You'll change the suggested name (Customer Query) to "Customer List."

3. Click at the end of the highlighted name, use the Backspace key to delete the word "Query," and then type **List**. You can now view the query results.

4. Click the **Finish** button to complete the query. Access displays the query results in Datasheet view.

5. Click the **Maximize** button ⟦▫⟧ on the Query window to maximize the window. See Figure 1-11.

Figure 1-11 ◀
Query results

selected fields
displayed

all 38 records are
included in the results

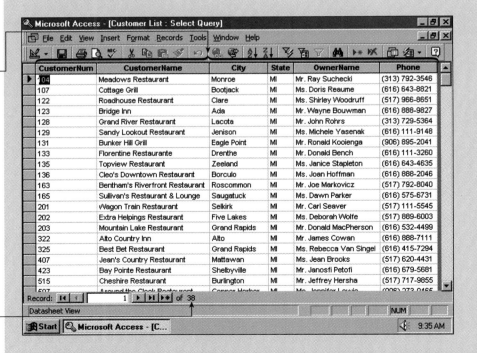

The datasheet displays the six selected fields for each record in the Customer table. The fields are shown in the order you selected them, from left to right.

The records are currently listed in order by the primary key field (CustomerNum). Kim prefers the records to be listed in order by state so that her staff members can focus on all the customers in a particular state. To display the records in the order Kim wants, you need to sort the query results by the State field.

To sort the query results:

1. Click to position the insertion point anywhere in the State column. This establishes the State column as the current field.

2. Click the **Sort Ascending** button 🔼 on the Query Datasheet toolbar. The records are now sorted in ascending alphabetical order by the values in the State field. All the records for Indiana are listed first, followed by the records for Michigan and then Ohio.

Kim asks for a printed copy of the query results so that she can bring the customer list to a meeting with her staff members. To print the query results, you can use the Print button on the Query Datasheet toolbar.

To print the query results:

1. Click the **Print** button 🖨 on the Query Datasheet toolbar to print one copy of the query results with the current settings.

2. Click the **Close** button ☒ on the menu bar to close the query.

   A dialog box opens asking if you want to save changes to the design of the query. This box appears because you changed the sort order of the query results.

3. Click the **Yes** button to save the changed query design and return to the Database window. Notice that the Customer List query is now shown in the Queries list box. In addition, because you had maximized the Query window, the Database window is also now maximized. You need to restore the window.

4. Click the **Restore** button 🗗 on the menu bar to restore the Database window.

The results of the query are not stored with the database; however, the query design is stored as part of the database with the name you specify. You can then re-create the query results at any time by running the query again. You'll learn more about creating and running queries in Tutorial 3.

After Kim leaves for her staff meeting, Barbara asks you to create a form for the Customer table so that her staff members can use the form to enter and work with data easily in the table.

Creating and Printing a Form

A **form** is an object you use to maintain, view, and print records in a database. Although you can perform these same functions with tables and queries, forms can present data in customized and useful ways.

In Access, you can design your own forms or use a Form Wizard to create forms for you automatically. A **Form Wizard** is an Access tool that asks you a series of questions, then creates a form based on your answers. The quickest way to create a form is to use an **AutoForm Wizard**, which places all the fields from a selected table (or query) on a form automatically, without asking you any questions, and then displays the form on the screen.

Barbara wants a form for the Customer table that will show all the fields for one record at a time, with fields listed one below another. This type of form will make it easier for her staff to focus on all the data for a particular customer. You'll use the AutoForm: Columnar Wizard to create the form.

To create the form using an AutoForm Wizard:

1. Click the **Forms** tab in the Database window to display the Forms list. The Forms list box is currently empty because you haven't created any forms yet.

2. Click the **New** button to open the New Form dialog box. See Figure 1-12.

Figure 1-12 ◄
New Form
dialog box

click to design your
own form

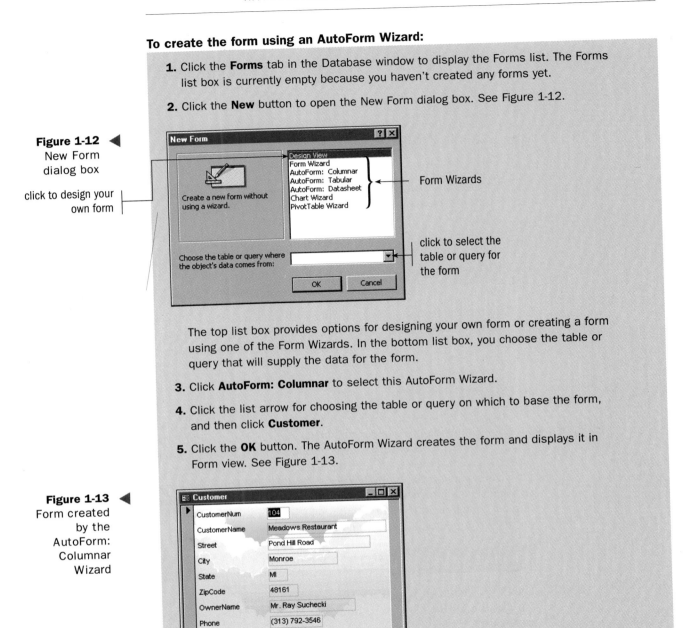

Form Wizards

click to select the
table or query for
the form

The top list box provides options for designing your own form or creating a form using one of the Form Wizards. In the bottom list box, you choose the table or query that will supply the data for the form.

3. Click **AutoForm: Columnar** to select this AutoForm Wizard.

4. Click the list arrow for choosing the table or query on which to base the form, and then click **Customer**.

5. Click the **OK** button. The AutoForm Wizard creates the form and displays it in Form view. See Figure 1-13.

Figure 1-13 ◄
Form created
by the
AutoForm:
Columnar
Wizard

The form displays one record at a time in the Customer table. Access displays the field values for the first record in the table and selects the first field value (CustomerNum). Each field name appears on a separate line and on the same line as its field value, which appears in a box. The widths of the boxes are different to accommodate the different sizes of the displayed field values; for example, compare the small box for the State field's value with the larger box for the CustomerName field's value. The AutoForm: Columnar Wizard automatically placed the field names and values on the form and supplied the background style.

Also, notice that the Form window contains navigation buttons, similar to those available in Datasheet view, which you can use to move to different records in the table.

Barbara asks you to print the data for the Embers Restaurant, which is the last record in the table. After printing this record in the form, you'll save the form with the name "Customer Data" in the Restaurant database. The form will then be available for later use. You'll learn more about creating and customizing forms in Tutorial 4.

To print the form with data for the last record, and then save and close the form:

1. Click the **Last Record** navigation button ⏭. The last record in the table, record 38 for Embers Restaurant, is now the current record.

2. Click **File** on the menu bar, and then click **Print**. The Print dialog box opens.

3. Click the **Selected Record(s)** option button, and then click the **OK** button to print only the current record in the form.

4. Click the **Save** button 💾 on the Form View toolbar. The Save As dialog box opens.

5. In the Form Name text box, click at the end of the highlighted word "Customer," press the **spacebar**, type **Data**, and then press the **Enter** key. Access saves the form as Customer Data in your Restaurant database and closes the dialog box.

6. Click the **Close** button ✖ on the Form window title bar to close the form and return to the Database window. Note that the Customer Data form is now listed in the Forms list box.

Kim returns from her staff meeting with another request. She wants the same customer list you produced earlier when you created the Customer List query, but she'd like the information presented in a more readable format. She suggests you use the Access Help system to learn about formatting data in reports.

Getting Help

The Access Help system provides the same options as the Help system in other Windows programs—the Help Contents, the Help Index, and the Find Feature, which are available on the Help menu. The Access Help system also provides additional ways to get help as you work—the Office Assistant and the What's This? command. You'll learn how to use the Office Assistant next in this section. The What's This? 💬 command provides context-sensitive Help information. When you choose this command from the Help menu, the pointer changes to the Help pointer, which you can then use to click any object or option on the screen to see a description of the object.

Finding Information with the Office Assistant

The Office Assistant is an interactive guide to finding information in the Help system. You can ask the Office Assistant a question, and it will look through the Help system to find an answer.

REFERENCE window	**USING THE OFFICE ASSISTANT**
	■ Click the Office Assistant button on any toolbar (or choose Microsoft Access Help from the Help menu). ■ Click in the text box, type your question, and then click the Search button. ■ Choose a topic from the list of topics displayed by the Office Assistant. Click additional topics, as necessary. ■ When finished, close the Help window and the Office Assistant.

You'll use the Office Assistant to get Help about creating reports in Access.

To get Help about reports:

1. Click the **Office Assistant** button 💬 on the Database toolbar. The Office Assistant appears and displays a dialog box with several options. See Figure 1-14.

Access

Figure 1-14 ◀
Office
Assistant

list of topics ——

type your question
in this text box

click to have Office
Assistant search
for an answer

Office
Assistant
window

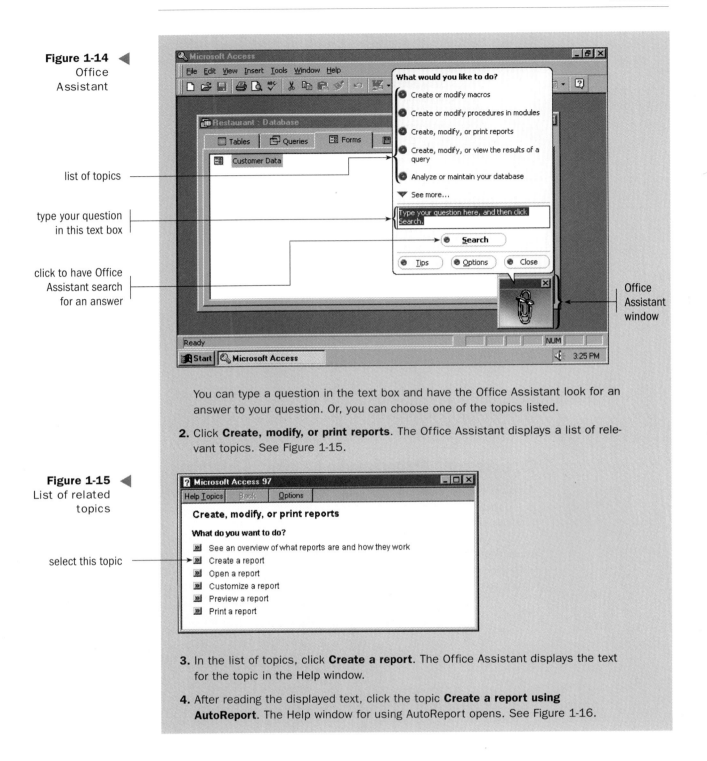

You can type a question in the text box and have the Office Assistant look for an answer to your question. Or, you can choose one of the topics listed.

2. Click **Create, modify, or print reports**. The Office Assistant displays a list of relevant topics. See Figure 1-15.

Figure 1-15 ◀
List of related
topics

select this topic ——

3. In the list of topics, click **Create a report**. The Office Assistant displays the text for the topic in the Help window.

4. After reading the displayed text, click the topic **Create a report using AutoReport**. The Help window for using AutoReport opens. See Figure 1-16.

Figure 1-16 ◀
Help
information on
AutoReport

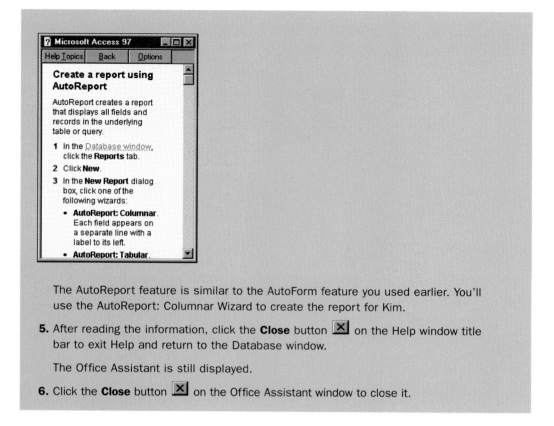

The AutoReport feature is similar to the AutoForm feature you used earlier. You'll use the AutoReport: Columnar Wizard to create the report for Kim.

5. After reading the information, click the **Close** button 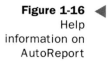 on the Help window title bar to exit Help and return to the Database window.

The Office Assistant is still displayed.

6. Click the **Close** button ☒ on the Office Assistant window to close it.

Creating, Previewing, and Printing a Report

A **report** is a formatted printout (or screen display) of the contents of one or more tables in a database. Although you can print data from tables, queries, and forms, reports allow you the greatest flexibility for formatting printed output.

Kim wants a report showing the same information as in the Customer List query you created earlier. However, she'd like the data for each customer to be grouped together, with one customer record below another, as shown in the report sketch in Figure 1-17. You'll use the AutoReport: Columnar Wizard to produce the report for Kim.

Figure 1-17 ◄
Sketch of
Kim's report

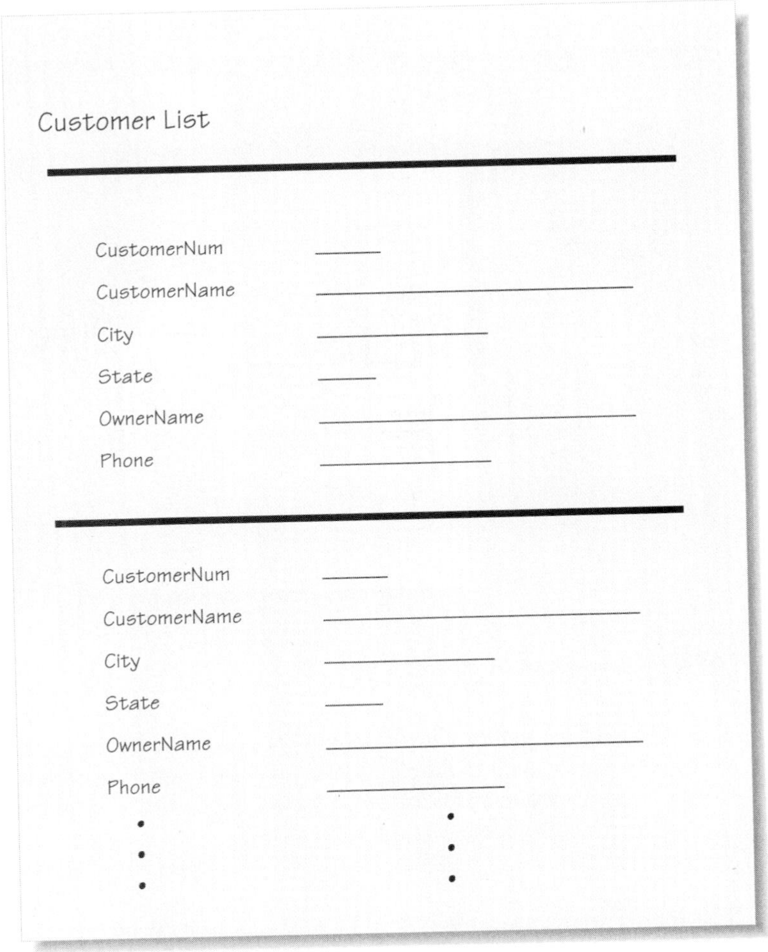

Customer List

CustomerNum   ———
CustomerName   ————————————
City   ——————————
State   ————
OwnerName   ————————————
Phone   ——————————

CustomerNum   ———
CustomerName   ————————————
City   ——————————
State   ————
OwnerName   ————————————
Phone   ——————————
     •   •
     •   •
     •   •

To create the report using the AutoReport: Columnar Wizard:

1. Click the **Reports** tab in the Database window, and then click the **New** button to open the New Report dialog box. This dialog box is similar to the New Form dialog box you saw earlier.

2. Click **AutoReport: Columnar** to select this wizard for creating the report.

   Because Kim wants the same data as in the Customer List query, you need to choose that query as the basis for the report.

3. Click the list arrow for choosing the table or query on which to base the report, and then click **Customer List**.

4. Click the **OK** button. The AutoReport Wizard creates the report and displays it in Print Preview, which shows exactly how the report will look when printed.

   To better view the report, you'll maximize the window and change the Zoom setting so that you can see the entire page.

5. Click the **Maximize** button 🔲 on the Report window, click the **Zoom** list arrow (next to the value 100%) on the Print Preview toolbar, and then click **Fit**. The entire first page of the report is displayed in the window. See Figure 1-18.

Figure 1-18 ◀
First page of
the report in
Print Preview

report title taken from
query name

fields grouped for
each record

lines
separate
records

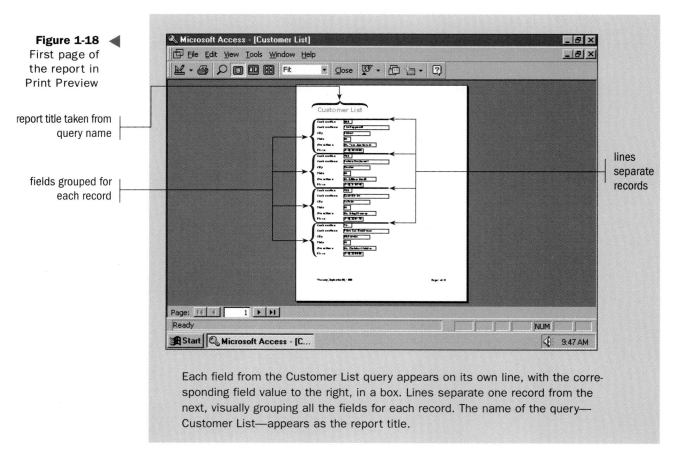

Each field from the Customer List query appears on its own line, with the corresponding field value to the right, in a box. Lines separate one record from the next, visually grouping all the fields for each record. The name of the query—Customer List—appears as the report title.

The report spans multiple pages. Kim asks you to print just the first page of the report so that she can review its format. After printing the report page, you'll close the report without saving it, because you can easily re-create it at any time. In general, it's best to save an object—report, form, or query—only if you anticipate using the object frequently or if it is time-consuming to create, because these objects can take up considerable storage space on your disk. You'll learn more about creating and customizing reports in Tutorial 4.

To print the first report page, and then close the report and exit Access:

1. Click **File** on the menu bar, and then click **Print**. The Print dialog box opens. You need to change the print settings so that only the first page of the report is printed.

2. In the Print Range section, click the **Pages** option button, type **1** in the From text box, press the **Tab** key, and then type **1** in the To text box.

3. Click the **OK** button to print the first page of the report. Now you can close the report.

4. Click the **Close** button ☒ on the menu bar. *Do not* click the Close button on the Print Preview toolbar.

   TROUBLE? If you clicked the Close button on the Print Preview toolbar, you switched to Design view. Simply click the Close button ☒ on the menu bar, and then continue with the tutorial.

   A dialog box opens asking if you want to save the changes to the report design.

5. Click the **No** button to close the report without saving it. Now you can exit Access.

6. Click the **Close** button ☒ on the Access window title bar to exit Access.

Quick Check

1 A(n) _____ is a question you ask about the data stored in a database.

2 Unless you specify otherwise, the records resulting from a query are listed in order by the _____.

3 The quickest way to create a form is to use a(n) _____.

4 Describe the form created by the AutoForm: Columnar Wizard.

5 Describe how you use the Office Assistant to get Help.

6 After creating a report, the AutoReport Wizard displays the report in _____.

With the Customer table in place, Barbara can continue to build the Restaurant database and use it to store, manipulate, and retrieve important data for Valle Coffee. In the following tutorials, you'll help Barbara complete and maintain the database, and you'll use it to meet the specific information needs of other Valle Coffee employees.

Tutorial Assignments

In the Tutorial Assignments, you'll work with the Customer database, which is similar to the database you worked with in the tutorial. Complete the following:

1. Make sure your Student Disk is in the disk drive.

2. Start Access and open the Customer database, which is located in the TAssign folder on your Student Disk.

3. Choose the Contents and Index command from the Help menu, and then select the Contents tab. Open the topic "Introduction to Microsoft Access 97" and then open the topic "Databases: What they are and how they work." Read the displayed information, and then click the >> button at the top of the window to move through the remaining screens for the topic. When finished, click the Help Topics button at the top of the window to return to the Contents tab. Repeat this procedure for the similarly worded topics for tables, queries, forms, and reports. On any screen that contains boxed items, click each item and read the information displayed in the pop-up window. When finished reading all the topics, close the Help window.

4. Use the Office Assistant to ask the following question: "How do I rename a table?" Choose the topic "Rename a table, query, form, report, macro, or module" and read the displayed information. Close the Help window and the Office Assistant. Then, in the Customer database, rename the Table1 table as Customers.

5. Open the Customers table.

6. Choose the Contents and Index command from the Help menu, and then select the Index tab. Look up the word "landscape," and then choose the topic "landscape page orientation." Choose the subtopic "Set margins, page orientation, and other page setup options." Read the displayed information, and then close the Help window. Print the Customers table datasheet in landscape orientation. Close the Customers table.

7. Use the Simple Query Wizard to create a query that includes the CustomerName, OwnerName, and Phone fields from the Customers table. Name the query Customer Phone List. Sort the query results in ascending order by CustomerName. Print the query results, and then close and save the query.

8. Use the AutoForm: Columnar Wizard to create a form for the Customers table.

9. Use context-sensitive Help to find out how to move to a particular record and display it in the form. Choose the What's This? command from the Help menu, and then use the Help pointer to click the number 1 in the Specific Record box at the bottom of the form. Read the displayed information. Click to close the Help box, and then use the Specific Record box to move to record 20 (for Cheshire Restaurant) in the Customers table.

10. Print the form for the current record (20), save the form as Customer Info, and then close the form.

11. Use the AutoReport: Tabular Wizard to create a report based on the Customers table. Print the first page of the report, and then close the report without saving it.

12. Exit Access.

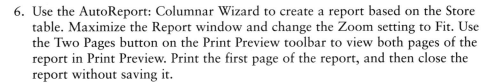

Case Problems

1. Ashbrook Mall Information Desk Ashbrook Mall is a large, modern mall located in Phoenix, Arizona. The Mall Operations Office is responsible for everything that happens within the mall and anything that affects the mall's operation. Among the independent operations that report to the Mall Operations Office are the Maintenance Group, the Mall Security Office, and the Information Desk. You will be helping the personnel at the Information Desk.

One important service provided by the Information Desk is to maintain a catalog of current job openings at stores within the mall. Sam Bullard, the director of the Mall Operations Office, recently created an Access database named MallJobs to store this information. You'll help Sam complete and maintain this database. Complete the following:

1. Make sure your Student Disk is in the disk drive.

2. Start Access and open the MallJobs database, which is located in the Cases folder on your Student Disk.

3. Open the Store table, print the table datasheet, and then close the table.

4. Use the Simple Query Wizard to create a query that includes the StoreName, Contact, and Extension fields from the Store table. Name the query Contact Phone List. Print the query results, and then close the query.

5. Use the AutoForm: Tabular Wizard to create a form for the Store table. Print the form, and then close it without saving it.

6. Use the AutoReport: Columnar Wizard to create a report based on the Store table. Maximize the Report window and change the Zoom setting to Fit. Use the Two Pages button on the Print Preview toolbar to view both pages of the report in Print Preview. Print the first page of the report, and then close the report without saving it.

7. Exit Access.

2. Professional Litigation User Services Professional Litigation User Services (PLUS) is a company that creates all types of visual aids for judicial proceedings. Clients are usually private law firms, although the District Attorney's office has occasionally contracted for their services. PLUS creates graphs, maps, timetables, and charts, both for computerized presentations and in large-size form for presentation to juries. PLUS also creates videos, animations, presentation packages, slide shows—in short, anything of a visual nature that can be used in a judicial proceeding to make, clarify, or support a point.

Raj Jawahir, a new employee at PLUS, is responsible for tracking the daily payments received from the firm's clients. He created an Access database named Payments, and needs your help in working with this database. Complete the following:

1. Make sure your Student Disk is in the disk drive.

2. Start Access and open the Payments database, which is located in the Cases folder on your Student Disk.

3. Open the Firm table, print the table datasheet, and then close the table.

4. Use the Simple Query Wizard to create a query that includes the FirmName, PLUSAcctRep, and Extension fields from the Firm table. Name the query Rep List. Sort the results in ascending order by the PLUSAcctRep field.

5. Use the Office Assistant to ask the following question: "How do I select multiple records?" Choose the topic "Selecting fields and records in Datasheet view," read the displayed information, and then close the Help window and the Office Assistant. Then select the first 11 records in the datasheet (all the records with the value "Abelson, David" in the PLUSAcctRep field), and then print just the selected records. Close the query, saving the changes to the design.

6. Use the AutoForm: Columnar Wizard to create a form for the Firm table. Move to record 31, and then print the form for the current record only. Close the form without saving it.

7. Use the AutoReport: Columnar Wizard to create a report based on the Firm table. Maximize the Report window and change the Zoom setting to Fit.

8. Use the View menu to view all eight pages of the report at the same time in Print Preview.

9. Print just the first page of the report, and then close the report without saving it.

10. Exit Access.

3. Best Friends Best Friends is a not-for-profit organization that trains hearing and service dogs for people with disabilities. Established in 1989 in Boise, Idaho, by Noah and Sheila Warnick, Best Friends is modeled after Paws With A Cause®, the original and largest provider of hearing and service dogs in the United States. Like Paws With A Cause® and other such organizations, Best Friends strives to provide "Dignity Through Independence."

To raise funds for Best Friends, Noah and Sheila periodically conduct Walk-A-Thons. The events have become so popular, Noah and Sheila created an Access database named Walks to track walker and pledge data. You'll help them complete and maintain the Walks database. Complete the following:

1. Make sure your Student Disk is in the disk drive.

2. Start Access and open the Walks database, which is located in the Cases folder on your Student Disk.

3. Open the Walker table, print the table datasheet, and then close the table.

4. Use the Simple Query Wizard to create a query that includes all the fields in the Walker table *except* the Phone field. (*Hint:* Use the >> and < buttons to select the necessary fields.) In the second Simple Query Wizard dialog box, make sure the Detail option button is selected. (This second dialog box appears because the table contains numeric values.) Name the query "Walker Distance." Sort the results in ascending order by the LastName field. Print the query results, and then close and save the query.

5. Use the AutoForm: Columnar Wizard to create a form for the Walker table. Move to record 25, and then print the form for the current record only. Close the form without saving it.

6. Use the AutoReport: Columnar Wizard to create a report based on the Walker table. Maximize the Report window and change the Zoom setting to Fit.

7. Use the View menu to view all six pages of the report at the same time in Print Preview.

8. Print just the first page of the report, and then close the report without saving it.

9. Exit Access.

4. Lopez Lexus Dealerships Maria and Hector Lopez own a chain of Lexus dealerships throughout Texas. They have used a computer in their business for several years to handle payroll and typical accounting functions. Because of their phenomenal expansion, both in the number of car locations and the number of cars handled, they created an Access database named Lexus to track their car inventory. You'll help them work with and maintain this database. Complete the following:

1. Make sure your Student Disk is in the disk drive.

2. Start Access and open the Lexus database, which is located in the Cases folder on your Student Disk.

3. Open the Cars table.

4. Print the Cars table datasheet in landscape orientation, and then close the table.

5. Use the Simple Query Wizard to create a query that includes the Model, Year, LocationCode, Cost, and SellingPrice fields from the Cars table. In the second Simple Query Wizard dialog box, make sure the Detail option button is selected. (This second dialog box appears because the table contains numeric values.) Name the query "Cost vs Selling."

6. Sort the query results in descending order by SellingPrice. (*Hint:* Use a toolbar button.)

7. Print the query results, and then close and save the query.

8. Use the AutoForm: Columnar Wizard to create a form for the Cars table. Move to record 11, and then print the form for the current record only. Close the form without saving it.

9. Use the AutoReport: Tabular Wizard to create a report based on the Cars table. Maximize the Report window and change the Zoom setting to Fit. Use the Two Pages button on the Print Preview toolbar to view both pages of the report in Print Preview. Print the first page of the report, and then close the report without saving it.

10. Exit Access.

Lab Assignments

These Lab Assignments are designed to accompany the interactive Course Lab called Databases. To start the Databases Lab, click the Start button on the Windows 95 taskbar, point to Programs, point to Course Labs, point to New Perspectives Applications, and click Databases. If you do not see Course Labs on your Programs menu, see your instructor or technical support person.

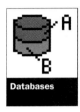

Databases

Databases This Databases Lab demonstrates the essential concepts of file and database management systems. You will use the Lab to search, sort, and report the data contained in a file of classic books.

1. Click the Steps button to review basic database terminology and to learn how to manipulate the classic books database. As you proceed through the Steps, answer all of the Quick Check questions that appear. After you complete the Steps, you will see a Quick Check summary report. Follow the instructions on the screen to print this report.

2. Click the Explore button. Make sure you can apply basic database terminology to describe the classic books database by answering the following questions:
   a. How many records does the file contain?
   b. How many fields does each record contain?
   c. What are the contents of the Catalog # field for the book written by Margaret Mitchell?
   d. What are the contents of the Title field for the record with Thoreau in the Author field?
   e. Which field has been used to sort the records?

3. In Explore, manipulate the database as necessary to answer the following questions:
   a. When the books are sorted by title, what is the first record in the file?
   b. Use the Search button to search for all the books in the West location. How many do you find?
   c. Use the Search button to search for all the books in the Main location that are checked in. What do you find?

4. Use the Report button to print out a report that groups the books by Status and sorts them by Title. On your report, circle the four field names. Draw a box around the summary statistics showing which books are currently checked in and which books are currently checked out.

Maintaining a Database

Creating, Modifying, and Updating an Order Table

Valle Coffee

CASE The Restaurant database currently contains only one table—the Customer table—which stores data about Valle Coffee's restaurant customers. Barbara also wants to track information about each order placed by each restaurant customer. This information includes the order's billing date and invoice amount. Barbara asks you to create a second table in the Restaurant database, named Order, in which to store the order data.

Some of the order data Barbara needs is already stored in another Valle Coffee database. After creating the Order table and adding some records to it, you'll copy the records from the other database into the Order table. Then you'll maintain the Order table by modifying it and updating it to meet Barbara's specific data requirements.

OBJECTIVES

In this tutorial you will:

- Learn the guidelines for designing databases and Access tables

- Create and save a table

- Define fields and specify the primary key

- Add records to a table

- Modify the structure of a table

- Delete, move, and add fields

- Change field properties

- Copy records from another Access database

- Delete and change records

SESSION 2.1 *In this session you will learn the guidelines for designing databases and Access tables. You'll also learn how to create a table, define the fields for a table, select the primary key for a table, save the table structure, and add records to a table datasheet.*

Guidelines for Designing Databases

A database management system can be a useful tool, but only if you first carefully design the database so that it meets the needs of those who will use it. In database design, you determine the fields, tables, and relationships needed to satisfy the data and processing requirements. When you design a database, you should follow these guidelines:

- **Identify all the fields needed to produce the required information.** For example, Barbara needs information about customers and orders. Figure 2-1 shows the fields that satisfy those information requirements.

Figure 2-1 ◀
Barbara's data requirements

CustomerName	BillingDate
OrderNum	OwnerName
Street	InvoiceAmt
City	PlacedBy
State	Phone
ZipCode	FirstContact
CustomerNum	

- **Group related fields into tables.** For example, Barbara grouped the fields relating to customers into the Customer table. The other fields are grouped logically into the Order table, which you will create, as shown in Figure 2-2.

Figure 2-2 ◀
Barbara's fields grouped into Customer and Order tables

Customer table	Order table
CustomerNum	OrderNum
CustomerName	BillingDate
Street	PlacedBy
City	InvoiceAmt
State	
ZipCode	
OwnerName	
Phone	
FirstContact	

- **Determine each table's primary key.** Recall that a primary key uniquely identifies each record in a table. Although a primary key is not mandatory in Access, it's usually a good idea to include one in each table. Without a primary key, selecting the exact record you want can be a problem. For some tables, one of the fields, such as a Social Security number or credit card number, naturally serves the function of a primary key. For other tables, two or more fields might be needed to function as the primary key. In these cases, the primary key is referred to as a **composite key**. For example, a school grade table would use a combination of student number and course code to serve as the primary key. For a third category of tables, no single field or combination of fields can uniquely identify a record in a table. In these cases, you need to add a field whose sole purpose is to serve as the primary key.

For Barbara's tables, CustomerNum is the primary key for the Customer table, and OrderNum will be the primary key for the Order table.

■ **Include a common field in related tables.** You use the common field to connect one table logically with another table. For example, Barbara's Customer and Order tables will include the CustomerNum field as a common field. Recall that when you include the primary key from one table as a field in a second table to form a relationship, the field is called a foreign key in the second table; therefore, the CustomerNum field will be a foreign key in the Order table. With this common field, Barbara can find all orders placed by a customer; she can use the CustomerNum value for a customer and search the Order table for all orders with that CustomerNum value. Likewise, she can determine which customer placed a particular order by searching the Customer table to find the one record with the same CustomerNum value as the corresponding value in the Order table.

■ **Avoid data redundancy.** Data redundancy occurs when you store the same data in more than one place. With the exception of common fields to connect tables, you should avoid redundancy because it wastes storage space and can cause inconsistencies, if, for instance, you type a field value one way in one table and a different way in the same table or in a second table. Figure 2-3 shows an example of incorrect database design that illustrates data redundancy in the Order table; the Customer Name field is redundant and one value was entered incorrectly, in three different ways.

Figure 2-3 ◀
Incorrect
database
design with
data
redundancy

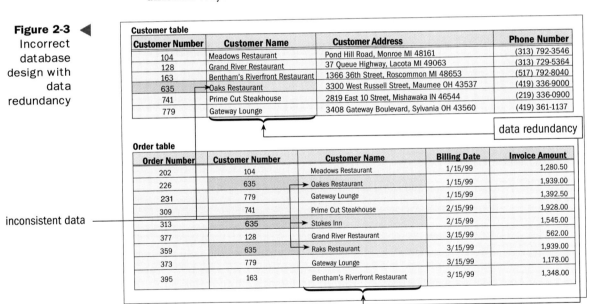

■ **Determine the properties of each field.** You need to identify the **properties**, or characteristics, of each field so that the DBMS knows how to store, display, and process the field. These properties include the field name, the field's maximum number of characters or digits, the field's description, the field's valid values, and other field characteristics. You will learn more about field properties later in this tutorial.

The Order table you need to create will contain the fields shown in Figure 2-2. Before you create the table, you first need to learn some guidelines for designing Access tables.

Guidelines for Designing Access Tables

As just noted, the last step of database design is to determine the properties, such as the name and data type, of each field. Access has rules for naming fields, choosing data types, and defining other properties for fields.

Naming Fields and Objects

You must name each field, table, and other object in an Access database. Access then stores these items in the database using the names you supply. It's best to choose a field or object name that describes the purpose or contents of the field or object, so that later you can easily remember what the name represents. For example, the two tables in the Restaurant database will be named Customer and Order, because these names suggest their contents.

The following rules apply to naming fields and objects:

- A name can be up to 64 characters long.

- A name can contain letters, numbers, spaces, and special characters except a period (.), exclamation mark (!), accent grave (`), and square brackets ([ ]).

- A name cannot start with a space.

- A table or query name must be unique within a database. A field name must be unique within a table, but it can be used again in another table.

In addition, experienced users of databases have the following tips for naming fields and objects:

- Capitalize the first letter of each word in the name.

- Avoid extremely long names because they are difficult to remember and refer to.

- Use standard abbreviations such as Num for Number, Amt for Amount, and Qty for Quantity.

- Do not use spaces in field names because these names will appear in column headings on datasheets and labels on forms and reports. By not using spaces you'll be able to show more fields on these objects at one time.

Assigning Field Data Types

You must assign a data type for each field. The **data type** determines what field values you can enter for the field and what other properties the field will have. For example, the Order table will include a BillingDate field, so you will assign the date/time data type to this field because it will store date values. Access will allow you to enter only dates or times as values for the field and will allow you to manipulate a value only as a date or time.

Figure 2-4 lists the ten data types available in Access, describes the field values allowed with each data type, explains when each data type should be used, and indicates the field size of each data type.

Figure 2-4 ◄
Data types
for fields

Data Type	Description	Field Size
Text	Allows field values containing letters, digits, spaces, and special characters. Use for names, addresses, descriptions, and fields containing digits that are not used in calculations.	1 to 255 characters; 50 characters default
Memo	Allows field values containing letters, digits, spaces, and special characters. Use for long comments and explanations.	1 to 64,000 characters; exact size is determined by entry
Number	Allows positive and negative numbers as field values. Numbers can contain digits, a decimal point, commas, a plus sign, and a minus sign. Use for fields that you will use in calculations, except calculations involving money.	1 to 15 digits
Date/Time	Allows field values containing valid dates and times from January 1, 100 to December 31, 9999. Dates can be entered in mm/dd/yy (month, day, year) format, several other date formats, or a variety of time formats such as 10:35 PM. You can perform calculations on dates and times and you can sort them. For example, you can determine the number of days between two dates.	8 digits
Currency	Allows field values similar to those for the number data type. Unlike calculations with number data type decimal values, calculations performed using the currency data type are not subject to round-off error.	15 digits
AutoNumber	Consists of integers with values controlled by Access. Access automatically inserts a value in the field as each new record is created. You can specify sequential numbering or random numbering. This guarantees a unique field value, so that such a field can serve as a table's primary key.	9 digits
Yes/No	Limits field values to yes and no, or true and false. Use for fields that indicate the presence or absence of a condition, such as whether an order has been filled, or if an employee is eligible for the company dental plan.	1 character
OLE Object	Allows field values that are created in other programs as objects, such as photographs, video images, graphics, drawings, sound recordings, voice-mail messages, spreadsheets, and word-processing documents. These objects can be linked or embedded.	1 gigabyte maximum; exact size depends on object size
Hyperlink	Consists of text or combinations of text and numbers stored as text and used as a hyperlink address. A hyperlink address can have up to three parts: the text that appears in a field or control; the path to a file or page; and a location within the file or page. Hyperlinks help you to connect your application easily to the Internet or an intranet.	Up to 2048 characters for each of the three parts of a hyperlink data type
Lookup Wizard	Creates a field that lets you look up a value in another table or in a predefined list of values.	Same size as the primary key field used to perform the lookup

Assigning Field Sizes

The **field size** property defines a field value's maximum storage size for text and number fields only. The other data types have no field size property, because their storage size is either a fixed, predetermined amount or is determined automatically by the field value itself, as shown in Figure 2-4. A text field has a default field size of 50 characters. You set its field size by entering a number in the range 1 to 255. For example, the OrderNum and CustomerNum fields in the Order table will be text fields with sizes of 3 each.

Barbara documented the design for the Order table by listing each field's name, data type, size (if applicable), and description, as shown in Figure 2-5. OrderNum, the table's primary key, CustomerNum, a foreign key to the Customer table, and PlacedBy will each be assigned the text data type. BillingDate will have the date/time data type, and InvoiceAmt will have the currency data type.

Figure 2-5 ◀
Design for the
Order table

Field Name	Data Type	Field Size	Description
OrderNum	Text	3	primary key
CustomerNum	Text	3	foreign key
BillingDate	Date/Time		
PlacedBy	Text	25	person who placed order
InvoiceAmt	Currency		

With Barbara's design, you are ready to create the Order table.

Creating a Table

Creating a table consists of naming the fields and defining the properties for the fields, specifying a primary key (and a foreign key, if applicable) for the table, and then saving the table structure. You will use Barbara's design (Figure 2-5) as a guide to creating the Order table. First, you need to open the Restaurant database.

To open the Restaurant database:

1. Place your Student Disk in the appropriate disk drive.

2. Start Access. The Access window opens with the initial dialog box.

3. Make sure the **Open an Existing Database** option button and the **More Files** option are selected, and then click the **OK** button to display the Open dialog box.

4. Click the **Look in** list arrow, and then click the drive that contains your Student Disk.

5. Click **Tutorial** in the list box, and then click the **Open** button to display a list of the files in the Tutorial folder.

6. Click **Restaurant** in the list box, and then click the **Open** button. The Restaurant database is displayed in the Access window.

7. Make sure the Tables tab is selected in the Database window.

The Customer table is listed in the Tables list box. Now you'll create the Order table in the Restaurant database.

To begin creating the Order table:

1. Click the **New** button in the Database window. The New Table dialog box opens. See Figure 2-6.

Access

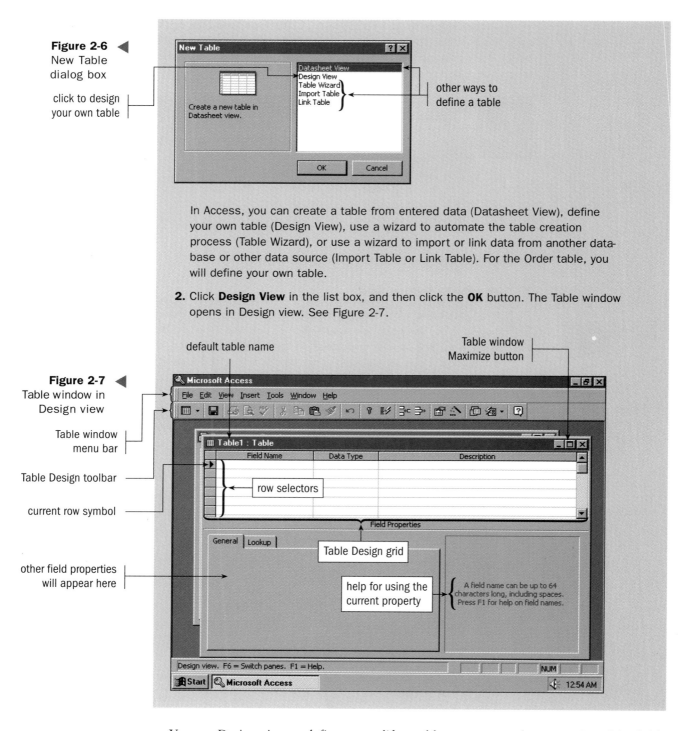

Figure 2-6 ◀
New Table
dialog box

click to design
your own table

other ways to
define a table

In Access, you can create a table from entered data (Datasheet View), define
your own table (Design View), use a wizard to automate the table creation
process (Table Wizard), or use a wizard to import or link data from another database or other data source (Import Table or Link Table). For the Order table, you
will define your own table.

2. Click **Design View** in the list box, and then click the **OK** button. The Table window
opens in Design view. See Figure 2-7.

default table name

Table window
Maximize button

Figure 2-7 ◀
Table window in
Design view

Table window
menu bar

Table Design toolbar

current row symbol

other field properties
will appear here

row selectors

Table Design grid

help for using the
current property

A field name can be up to 64
characters long, including spaces.
Press F1 for help on field names.

You use Design view to define or modify a table structure or the properties of the fields
in a table. If you create a table without using a wizard, you enter the fields and their properties for your table directly in this window.

Defining Fields

Initially, the default table name, Table1, appears in the Table window title bar, the current row symbol is positioned in the first row selector of the Table Design grid, and the
insertion point is located in the first row's Field Name box. The purpose or characteristics of the current property (Field Name, in this case) appear in the lower-right of the
Table window. You can display more complete information about the current property by
pressing the F1 key.

You enter values for the Field Name, Data Type, and Description field properties in the upper-half of the Table window. You select values for all other field properties, most of which are optional, in the lower-half of the window. These other properties will appear when you move to the first row's Data Type text box.

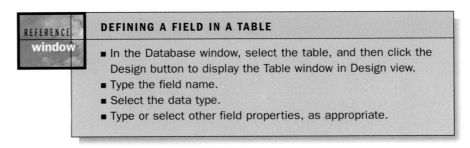

REFERENCE window

DEFINING A FIELD IN A TABLE

- In the Database window, select the table, and then click the Design button to display the Table window in Design view.
- Type the field name.
- Select the data type.
- Type or select other field properties, as appropriate.

The first field you need to define is OrderNum.

To define the OrderNum field:

1. Type **OrderNum** in the first row's Field Name text box, and then press the **Tab** key (or press the **Enter** key) to advance to the Data Type text box. The default data type, Text, appears highlighted in the Data Type text box, which now also contains a list arrow, and field properties for a text field appear in the lower-half of the window. See Figure 2-8.

Figure 2-8
Table window after entering the first field name

field name

default data type

properties for a text field

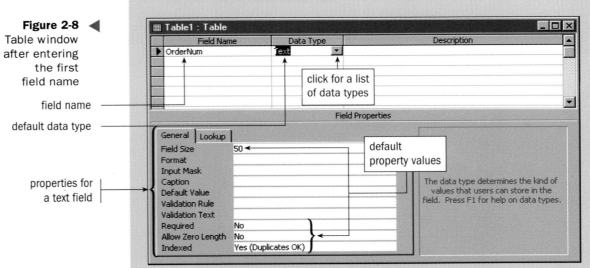

Notice that the lower-right of the window now provides an explanation for the current property, Data Type.

TROUBLE? If you make a typing error, you can correct it by clicking the mouse to position the insertion point, and then using either the Backspace key to delete characters to the left of the insertion point or the Delete key to delete characters to the right of the insertion point. Then type the correct text.

Because order numbers will not be used for calculations, you will assign the text data type to it instead of the number data type, and then enter the Description property value as "primary key." You can use the Description property to enter an optional description for a field to explain its purpose or usage. A field's Description property can be up to 255 characters long, and its value appears in the status bar when you view the table datasheet.

2. Press the **Tab** key to accept Text as the field's data type and move to the Description text box, and then type **primary key** in the Description text box.

The Field Size property has a default value of 50, which you will change to a value of 3, because order numbers at Valle Coffee contain 3 digits. The Required property has a default value of No, which means that a value does not need to be entered for the field. Because Barbara doesn't want an order entered without an order number, you will change the Required property to Yes. The Allow Zero Length property has a value of No, meaning that a value *must* be entered for the field, as is appropriate for the OrderNum field. Finally, the Indexed property has a value of "Yes (Duplicates OK)," which means that a list of index entries will be created to speed up operations using the OrderNum field.

3. Select **50** in the Field Size text box either by dragging the pointer or double-clicking the mouse, and then type **3**.

4. Click the **Required** text box to position the insertion point there. A list arrow appears on the right side of the Required text box.

5. Click the **Required** list arrow. Access displays the Required list box. See Figure 2-9.

Figure 2-9 ◄
Defining the
OrderNum field

changed from
default value of 50

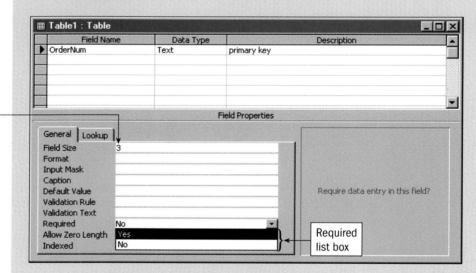

When you position the insertion point or select text in many Access text boxes, Access displays a list arrow, which you can click to display a list box with options. You can display the list arrow *and* the list box simultaneously if you click the text box near its right side.

6. Click **Yes** in the list box. The list box closes, and Yes is now the value for the Required property. The definition of the first field is complete.

Barbara's Order table design shows CustomerNum as the second field. You will define CustomerNum as a text field with a Description of "foreign key" and a Field Size of 3, because customer numbers at Valle Coffee contain 3 digits. Because it's possible that a record for an order might need to be entered for a customer not yet added to the database, Barbara asks you to leave the Required property at its default value of No and to change the Allow Zero Length property value to Yes.

To define the CustomerNum field:

1. Place the insertion point in the second row's Field Name text box, type **CustomerNum** in the text box, and then press the **Tab** key to advance to the Data Type text box.

Customer numbers are not used in calculations, so you'll assign the text data type to the field, and then enter its Description value as "foreign key."

2. Press the **Tab** key to accept Text as the field's data type and move to the Description text box, and then type **foreign key** in the Description text box.

   Finally, change the Field Size property to 3 and the Allow Zero Length property to Yes.

3. Select **50** in the Field Size text box, type **3**, click the right side of the Allow Zero Length text box, and then click **Yes**. You have completed the definition of the second field. See Figure 2-10.

Figure 2-10 ◀
Table window after defining the first two fields

current field

property values for the current field

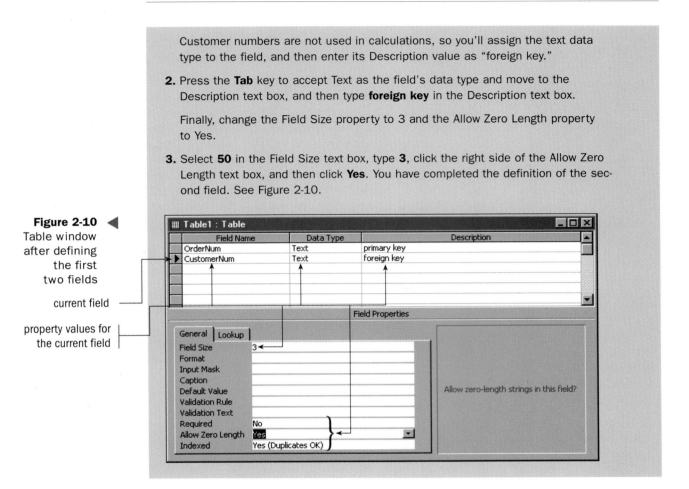

Using Barbara's Order table design in Figure 2-5, you can now complete the remaining field definitions: BillingDate with the date/time data type, PlacedBy with the text data type, and InvoiceAmt with the currency data type.

To define the BillingDate, PlacedBy, and InvoiceAmt fields:

1. Place the insertion point in the third row's Field Name text box, type **BillingDate** in the text box, and then press the **Tab** key to advance to the Data Type text box.

2. Click the **Data Type** list arrow, click **Date/Time** in the list box, and then press the **Tab** key to advance to the Description text box.

   If you've assigned a descriptive field name and the field does not fulfill a special function (for example, primary key), you usually do not enter a value for the optional Description property. BillingDate is a field that does not require a value for its Description property.

   Barbara does not want to require that a value be entered for the BillingDate field, nor does she want an index for the field. So, you do not need to change any of the default property values for the BillingDate field. Neither do you need to enter any new property values. Because you have finished defining the BillingDate field, you can now define the PlacedBy field.

3. Press the **Tab** key to advance to the fourth row's Field Name text box.

4. Type **PlacedBy** in the Field Name text box, and then press the **Tab** key to advance to the Data Type text box.

This field will contain names, so you'll assign the text data type to it. Also, Barbara wants to include the description "person who placed order" to clarify the contents of the field.

5. Press the **Tab** key to accept Text as the field's data type and move to the Description text box, and then type **person who placed order** in the Description text box.

Next, you'll change the Field Size property's default value of 50 to 25, which should be long enough to accommodate all names. Also, Barbara does not want to require that a value be entered for the field.

6. Select **50** in the Field Size text box, type **25**, click the right side of the Allow Zero Length text box, and then click **Yes**.

The definition of the PlacedBy field is complete. Next, you'll define the fifth and final field, InvoiceAmt. This field will contain dollar amounts so you'll assign the currency data type to it.

7. Place the insertion point in the fifth row's Field Name text box.

8. Type **InvoiceAmt** in the Field Name text box, and then press the **Tab** key to advance to the Data Type text box.

You can select a value from the Data Type list box as you did for the BillingDate field. Alternatively, you can type the property value in the text box or type just the first character of the property value.

9. Type **c**. The value in the fifth row's Data Type text box changes to "currency," with the letters "urrency" highlighted. See Figure 2-11.

Figure 2-11 ◄
Selecting a
value for the
Data Type
property

"c" typed ——————

"urrency"
automatically added
and highlighted

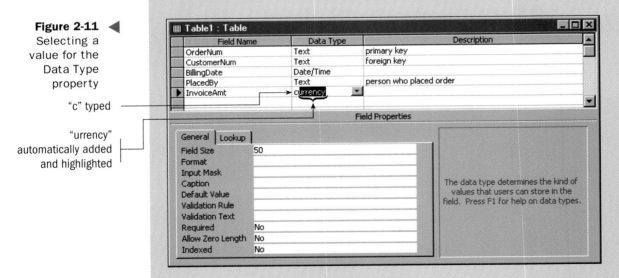

10. Press the **Tab** key to advance to the Description text box. Access changes the value for the Data Type property to Currency.

In the Field Properties section, notice the default values for the Format and Decimal Places properties. For a field with a Format property value of Currency, two decimal places are provided when the Decimal Places property value is Auto. This is the format Barbara wants for the InvoiceAmt field, so you have finished defining the fields for the Order table.

Next, you need to specify the primary key for the Order table.

Specifying the Primary Key

Although Access does not require a table to have a primary key, including a primary key offers several advantages:

- A primary key uniquely identifies each record in a table.

- Access does not allow duplicate values in the primary key field. If a record already exists with an OrderNum value of 143, for example, Access prevents you from adding another record with this same value in the OrderNum field. Preventing duplicate values ensures the uniqueness of the primary key field and helps to avoid data redundancy.

- Access forces you to enter a value for the primary key field in every record in the table. This is known as **entity integrity**. If you do not enter a value for a field, you have actually given the field what is known as a **null value**. You cannot give a null value to the primary key field because entity integrity prevents Access from accepting and processing that record.

- Access stores records on disk in the same order as you enter them but displays them in order by the field values of the primary key. If you enter records in no specific order, you are ensured that you will later be able to work with them in a more meaningful, primary key sequence.

- Access responds faster to your requests for specific records based on the primary key.

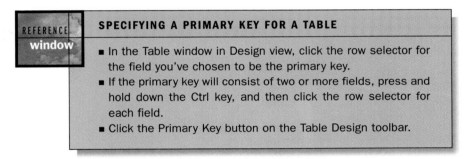

REFERENCE window	**SPECIFYING A PRIMARY KEY FOR A TABLE**
	■ In the Table window in Design view, click the row selector for the field you've chosen to be the primary key.
	■ If the primary key will consist of two or more fields, press and hold down the Ctrl key, and then click the row selector for each field.
	■ Click the Primary Key button on the Table Design toolbar.

According to Barbara's design, you need to specify OrderNum as the primary key for the Order table.

To specify OrderNum as the primary key:

1. Position the pointer on the row selector for the OrderNum field until the pointer changes to ➡. See Figure 2-12.

Primary Key button

Figure 2-12 ◀
Specifying
OrderNum as
the primary key

pointer ———

row selector ———

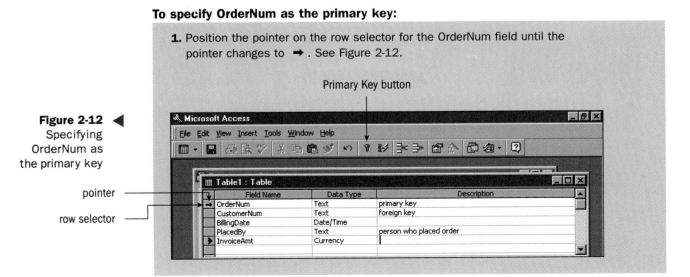

2. Click the mouse button. The entire first row of the Table Design grid is highlighted.

3. Click the **Primary Key** button 🔑 on the Table Design toolbar, and then click to the right of InvoiceAmt in the fifth row's Field Name text box to deselect the first row. A key symbol appears in the row selector for the first row, indicating that the OrderNum field is the table's primary key. See Figure 2-13.

Figure 2-13 ◄
OrderNum
selected as the
primary key

key symbol indicating
the primary key

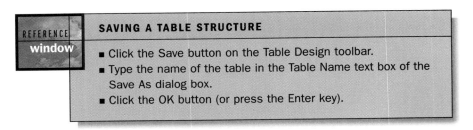

	Field Name	Data Type	Description
🔑	OrderNum	Text	primary key
	CustomerNum	Text	foreign key
	BillingDate	Date/Time	
	PlacedBy	Text	person who placed order
▶	InvoiceAmt	Currency	

You've defined the fields for the Order table and specified its primary key, so you can now save the table structure.

Saving the Table Structure

The last step in creating a table is to name the table and save the table's structure on disk. Once the table is saved, you can use it to enter data in the table.

> **REFERENCE window**
>
> **SAVING A TABLE STRUCTURE**
>
> - Click the Save button on the Table Design toolbar.
> - Type the name of the table in the Table Name text box of the Save As dialog box.
> - Click the OK button (or press the Enter key).

You need to save the table you've defined as "Order."

To name and save the Order table:

1. Click the **Save** button 💾 on the Table Design toolbar. The Save As dialog box opens.

2. Type **Order** in the Table Name text box, and then press the **Enter** key. Access saves the table with the name Order in the Restaurant database on your Student Disk. Notice that Order appears instead of Table1 in the Table window title bar.

Next, Barbara asks you to add two records, shown in Figure 2-14, to the Order table. These two records contain data for orders that were recently placed with Valle Coffee.

Figure 2-14 ◄
Records to be
added to the
Order table

OrderNum	CustomerNum	BillingDate	PlacedBy	InvoiceAmt
323	624	2/15/99	Isabelle Rouy	$1,986.00
201	107	1/15/99	Matt Gellman	$854.00

Adding Records to a Table

You can add records to an Access table in several ways. A table datasheet provides a simple way for you to add records. As you learned in Tutorial 1, a datasheet shows a table's contents in rows and columns, similar to a table or worksheet. Each row is a separate record in the table, and each column contains the field values for one field in the table. To view a table datasheet, you first must change from Design view to Datasheet view.

You'll switch to Datasheet view and add the two records in the Order table datasheet.

To add the records in the Order table datasheet:

1. Click the **View** button for Datasheet view 🔲 on the Table Design toolbar. The Table window opens in Datasheet view. See Figure 2-15.

Figure 2-15 ◄
Table window in
Datasheet view

current record symbol

field names

Description property
for the current field

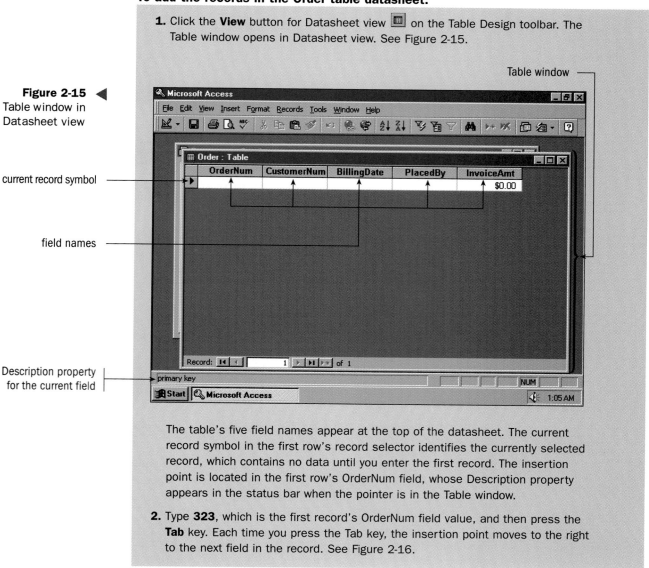

The table's five field names appear at the top of the datasheet. The current record symbol in the first row's record selector identifies the currently selected record, which contains no data until you enter the first record. The insertion point is located in the first row's OrderNum field, whose Description property appears in the status bar when the pointer is in the Table window.

2. Type **323**, which is the first record's OrderNum field value, and then press the **Tab** key. Each time you press the Tab key, the insertion point moves to the right to the next field in the record. See Figure 2-16.

Access

Figure 2-16 ◀
Datasheet for
Order table
after entering
the first
field value

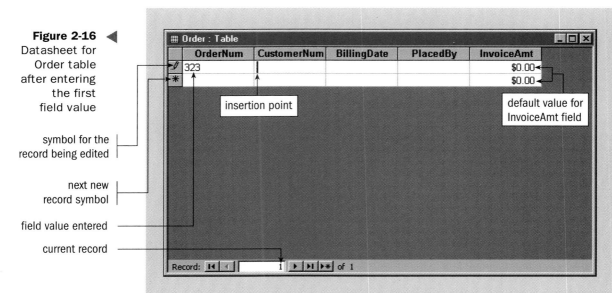

symbol for the
record being edited

next new
record symbol

field value entered

current record

TROUBLE? If you make a mistake when typing a value, use the Backspace key
to delete characters to the left of the insertion point or the Delete key to delete
characters to the right of the insertion point. Then type the correct text. If you
want to correct a value by replacing it entirely, double-click the value to select it,
and then type the correct value.

The pencil symbol in the first row's record selector indicates that the record is being
edited. The star symbol in the second row's record selector identifies the second
row as the next one available for a new record. The InvoiceAmt column displays
"$0.00," the default value for the field.

3. Type **624** and then press the **Tab** key. The insertion point moves to the right side
   of the BillingDate field.

4. Type **2/15/99** and then press the **Tab** key. The insertion point moves to the
   PlacedBy field.

5. Type **Isabelle Rouy** and then press the **Tab** key. The insertion point moves to the
   InvoiceAmt field, whose field value is highlighted.

Notice that field values for text fields are left-aligned in their boxes and field
values for date/time and currency fields are right-aligned in their boxes. If the
default value of $0.00 is correct for the InvoiceAmt field, you can press the
Tab key to accept the value and advance to the beginning of the next record.
Otherwise, type the field value for the InvoiceAmt field. You do not need to type
the dollar sign, commas, or decimal point (for whole dollar amounts) because
Access adds these symbols automatically for you.

6. Type **1986** and then press the **Tab** key. Access displays $1,986.00 for the
   InvoiceAmt field, stores the first completed record in the Order table, removes
   the pencil symbol from the first row's record selector, advances the insertion
   point to the second row's OrderNum text box, and places the current record
   symbol in the second row's record selector.

Now you can enter the values for the second record.

7. Type **201** in the OrderNum field, press the **Tab** key to move to the CustomerNum
   field, type **107** in the CustomerNum field, and then press the **Tab** key. The insertion point moves to the right side of the BillingDate field.

8. Type **1/15/99** and then press the **Tab** key. The insertion point moves to the
   PlacedBy field.

9. Type **Matt Gellman** and then press the **Tab** key. The value in the InvoiceAmt field is now highlighted.

10. Type **854** and then press the **Tab** key. Access changes the InvoiceAmt field value to $854.00, saves the record in the Order table, and moves the insertion point to the beginning of the third row. See Figure 2-17.

Figure 2-17 ◄
Order table
datasheet after
entering the
second record

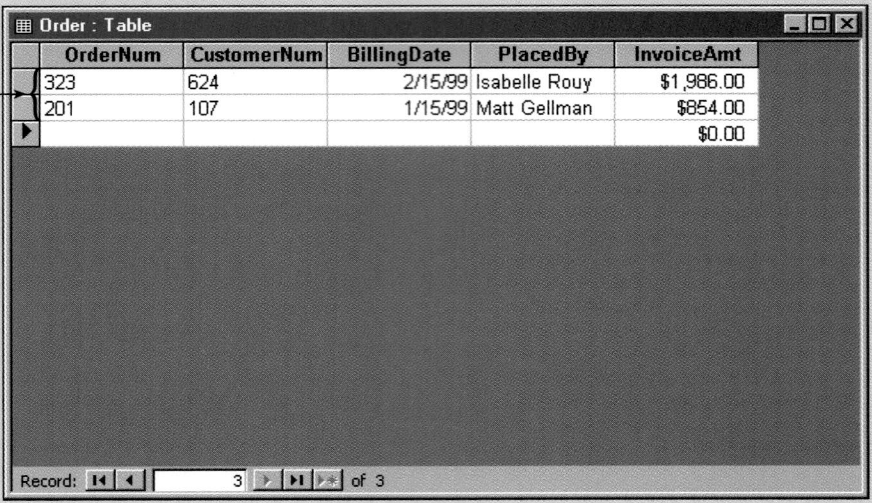

two added records ─

	OrderNum	CustomerNum	BillingDate	PlacedBy	InvoiceAmt
	323	624	2/15/99	Isabelle Rouy	$1,986.00
	201	107	1/15/99	Matt Gellman	$854.00
►					$0.00

Record: ◄◄ ◄ 3 ► ►◄ ►* of 3

Notice that "Record 3 of 3" appears around the navigation buttons even though the table contains only two records. Access is anticipating that you will enter a new record, which would be the third of three records in the table. If you move the insertion point to the second record, the display would change to "Record 2 of 2."

Even though the Order table contains only two records, Barbara asks you to print the table datasheet so that she can bring it with her to a staff meeting. She wants to show the table design to her staff members to make sure that it will meet their needs for tracking order data.

You'll use the Print button on the Table Datasheet toolbar to print one copy of the Order table with the current settings.

To print the Order table:

1. Click the **Print** button 🖨 on the Table Datasheet toolbar.

Notice that the two records are currently listed in the order in which you entered them. However, once you close the table or change to another view, and then redisplay the table datasheet, the records will be listed in primary key order by the values in the OrderNum field.

You have created the Order table in the Restaurant database and added two records to the table, which Access saved automatically to the database on your Student Disk.

Saving a Database

Notice the Save button on the Table Datasheet toolbar. This Save button, unlike the Save buttons in other Windows programs, does not save the active document (database) to your disk. Instead, you use the Save button to save the design of a table, query, form, or report, or to save datasheet format changes. Access does not have a button or option you can use to save the active database.

Access saves the active database to your disk automatically, both on a periodic basis and whenever you close the database. This means that if your database is stored on a disk in drive A or drive B, you should never remove the disk while the database file is open. If you do remove the disk, Access will encounter problems when it tries to save the database; this might damage the database.

Quick Check

1. What guidelines should you follow when you design a database?

2. What is the purpose of the data type property for a field?

3. For which two types of fields do you assign a field size?

4. Why did you define the OrderNum field as a text field instead of a number field?

5. A(n) _____ value, which results when you do not enter a value for a field, is not permitted for a primary key.

6. What does a pencil symbol in a datasheet's row selector represent? A star symbol?

The Order table is now complete. In Session 2.2, you'll continue to work with the Order table by modifying its structure and entering and maintaining data in the table.

SESSION 2.2

In this session you will modify the structure of a table by deleting, moving, and adding fields and changing field properties; copy records from another Access database; and update a database by deleting and changing records.

Modifying the Structure of an Access Table

Even a well-designed table might need to be modified. For example, the government at all levels and the competition place demands on a company to track more data and to modify the data it already tracks. Access allows you to modify a table's structure in Design view: you can add and delete fields, change the order of fields, and change the properties of the fields.

After meeting with her staff members and reviewing the structure of the Order table and the format of the field values in the datasheet, Barbara has several changes she wants you to make to the table. First, she has decided that it's not necessary to keep track of the name of the person who placed a particular order, so she wants you to delete the PlacedBy field. Also, she thinks that the InvoiceAmt field should remain a currency field, but she wants the dollar signs removed from the displayed field values in the datasheet. She also wants the BillingDate field moved to the end of the table. Finally, she wants you to add a yes/no field, named Paid, to the table to indicate whether the invoice has been paid for the order. The Paid field will be inserted between the CustomerNum and InvoiceAmt fields. Figure 2-18 shows Barbara's modified design for the Order table.

Figure 2-18 ◀
Modified design for the Order table

Field Name	Data Type	Field Size	Description
OrderNum	Text	3	primary key
CustomerNum	Text	3	foreign key
Paid	Yes/No		
InvoiceAmt	Currency		
BillingDate	Date/Time		

You'll begin modifying the table by deleting the PlacedBy field.

Deleting a Field

After you've defined a table structure and added records to the table, you can delete a field from the table structure. When you delete a field, you also delete all the values for the field from the table. Therefore, you should make sure that you need to delete a field and that you delete the correct field.

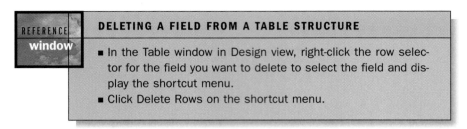

REFERENCE window

DELETING A FIELD FROM A TABLE STRUCTURE

- In the Table window in Design view, right-click the row selector for the field you want to delete to select the field and display the shortcut menu.
- Click Delete Rows on the shortcut menu.

You need to delete the PlacedBy field from the Order table structure.

To delete the PlacedBy field:

1. If you took a break after the previous session, make sure that Access is running and that the Order table of the Restaurant database is open.

2. Click the **View** button for Design view ![icon] on the Table Datasheet toolbar. The Table window for the Order table opens in Design view.

3. Position the pointer on the row selector for the PlacedBy field until the pointer changes to ➡ .

4. Right-click to select the entire row for the field and display the shortcut menu, and then click **Delete Rows**.

    A dialog box opens asking you to confirm the deletion.

5. Click the **Yes** button to close the dialog box and to delete the field and its values from the table. See Figure 2-19.

Figure 2-19 ◀
Table structure after deleting PlacedBy field

field deleted here

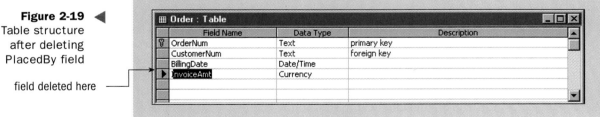

You have deleted the PlacedBy field in the Table window, but the change doesn't take place in the table on disk until you save the table structure. Because you have other modifications to make to the table, you'll wait until you finish them all before saving the modified table structure to disk.

Moving a Field

To move a field, you use the mouse to drag it to a new location in the Table window in Design view. Your next modification to the Order table structure is to move the BillingDate field to the end of the table, as Barbara requested.

To move the BillingDate field:

1. Click the **row selector** for the BillingDate field to select the entire row.

2. Place the pointer in the row selector for the BillingDate field, click the pointer ⌖ , and then drag the pointer ⌖ to the row selector below the InvoiceAmt row selector. See Figure 2-20.

Figure 2-20 ◀
Moving a field
in the table
structure

selected field ⎯

position the move
pointer in this
row selector ⎯

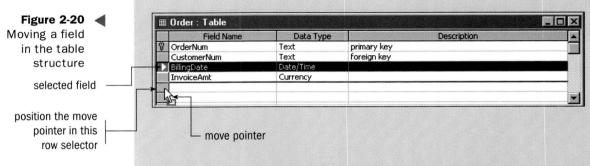

⎯ move pointer

3. Release the mouse button. Access moves the BillingDate field below the InvoiceAmt field in the table structure.

TROUBLE? If the BillingDate field did not move, repeat Steps 1 through 3, making sure you firmly hold down the mouse button during the drag operation.

Adding a Field

Next, you need to add the Paid field to the table structure between the CustomerNum and InvoiceAmt fields. To add a new field between existing fields, you must insert a row. You begin by selecting the field that will be below the new field you want to insert.

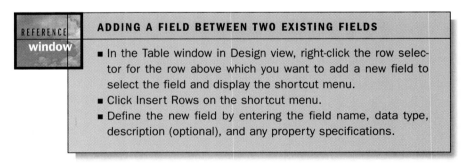

REFERENCE window

ADDING A FIELD BETWEEN TWO EXISTING FIELDS

- In the Table window in Design view, right-click the row selector for the row above which you want to add a new field to select the field and display the shortcut menu.
- Click Insert Rows on the shortcut menu.
- Define the new field by entering the field name, data type, description (optional), and any property specifications.

To add the Paid field to the Order table:

1. Right-click the **row selector** for the InvoiceAmt field to select this field and display the shortcut menu, and then click **Insert Rows**. Access adds a new, blank row between the CustomerNum and InvoiceAmt fields. See Figure 2-21.

Figure 2-21 ◀
After inserting
a row in the
table structure

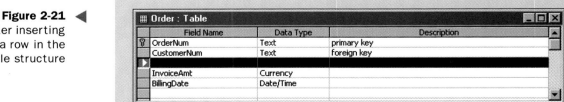

You'll define the Paid field in the new row for the Order table. Access will add this new field to the Order table structure between the CustomerNum and InvoiceAmt fields.

2. Click the **Field Name** text box for the new row, type **Paid**, and then press the **Tab** key.

The Paid field will be a yes/no field that will specify whether an invoice has been paid.

3. Type **y**. Access completes the data type as "yes/No."

4. Press the **Tab** key to select the yes/no data type and move to the Description text box.

Notice that Access changes the value in the Data Type text box from "yes/No" to "Yes/No." Barbara wants the Paid field to have a Default Value property value of "no." When you select or enter a value for a property, you *set* the property.

5. In the Field Properties section, click the **Default Value** text box, type **no**, and then click the **Description** text box for the Paid field. Notice that Access changes the Default Value property value from "no" to "No." See Figure 2-22.

Figure 2-22 ◄
Paid field
added to the
Order table

new field ───

Default Value │
property set to "No" │

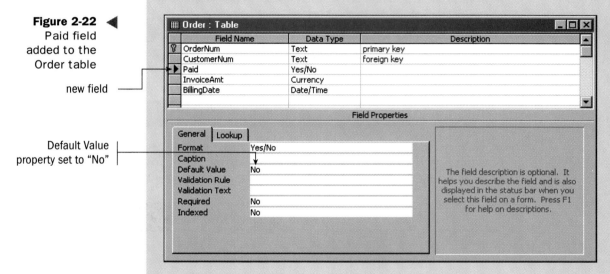

Because its field name clearly indicates its purpose, you do not need to enter a description for the Paid field.

You've completed adding the Paid field to the Order table in Design view. As with the other changes you've made, however, the Paid field is not added to the Order table in the Restaurant database until you save the changes to the table structure.

Changing Field Properties

Barbara's last modification to the table structure is to remove the dollar signs from the InvoiceAmt field values displayed in the datasheet, because repeated dollar signs are unnecessary and clutter the datasheet. You use the **Format property** to control the display of a field value.

To change the Format property of the InvoiceAmt field:

1. Click the **Description** text box for the InvoiceAmt field. The InvoiceAmt field is now the current field.

2. Click the **Format** text box in the Field Properties section, and then click the **Format** list arrow to display the Format list box. See Figure 2-23.

Figure 2-23 ◀
Format list box

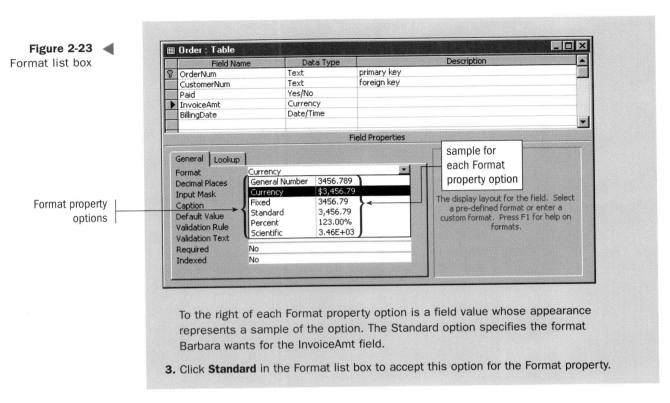

Format property
options

To the right of each Format property option is a field value whose appearance represents a sample of the option. The Standard option specifies the format Barbara wants for the InvoiceAmt field.

3. Click **Standard** in the Format list box to accept this option for the Format property.

Barbara wants you to add a third record to the Order table datasheet. Before you can add the record, you must save the modified table structure, and then switch to the Order table datasheet.

To save the modified table structure, and then switch to the datasheet:

1. Click the **Save** button 🖫 on the Table Design toolbar. The modified table structure for the Order table is stored in the Restaurant database.

2. Click the **View** button for Datasheet view 🔲 on the Table Design toolbar. The Order table datasheet opens. See Figure 2-24.

Figure 2-24 ◀
Datasheet for
the modified
Order table

records in primary
key order

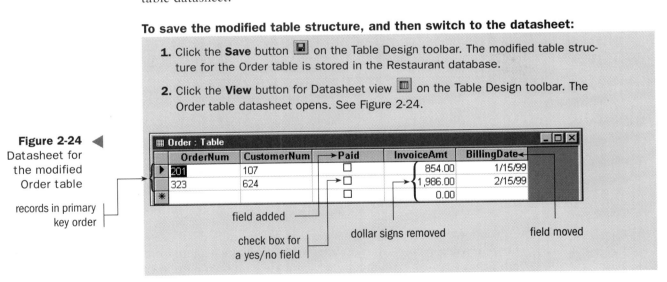

field added

check box for
a yes/no field

dollar signs removed

field moved

Notice that the PlacedBy field no longer appears in the datasheet, the BillingDate field is now the rightmost column, the InvoiceAmt field values do not contain dollar signs, and the Paid field appears between the CustomerNum and InvoiceAmt fields. The Paid column contains check boxes to represent the yes/no field values. Empty check boxes signify "No," which is the default value you assigned to the Paid field. A "Yes" value is indicated by a check mark in the check box. Also notice that the records appear in ascending order based on the value in the OrderNum field, the Order table's primary key, even though you did not enter the records in this order.

Barbara asks you to add a third record to the table. This record is for an order that has been paid.

To add the record to the modified Order table:

1. Click the **New Record** button ▶* on the Table Datasheet toolbar. The insertion point is located in the OrderNum field for the third row, which is the next row available for a new record.

2. Type **211**. The pencil symbol appears in the row selector for the third row, and the star appears in the row selector for the fourth row. Recall that these symbols represent a record being edited and the next available record, respectively.

3. Press the **Tab** key. The insertion point moves to the CustomerNum field.

4. Type **201** and then press the **Tab** key. The insertion point moves to the Paid field.

   Recall that the default value for this field is "No," which means the check box is initially empty. For yes/no fields with check boxes, you press the Tab key to leave the check box unchecked; you press the spacebar or click the check box to add or remove a check mark in the check box. Because the invoice for this order has been paid, you need to insert a check mark in the check box.

5. Press the **spacebar**. A check mark appears in the check box.

6. Press the **Tab** key. The value in the InvoiceAmt field is now highlighted.

7. Type **703.5** and then press the **Tab** key. The insertion point moves to the BillingDate field.

8. Type **1/15/99** and then press the **Tab** key. Access saves the record in the Order table and moves the insertion point to the beginning of the fourth row. See Figure 2-25.

Figure 2-25 ◀
Order table
datasheet
with third
record added

record added ———

"Yes" value ———

"No" values ———

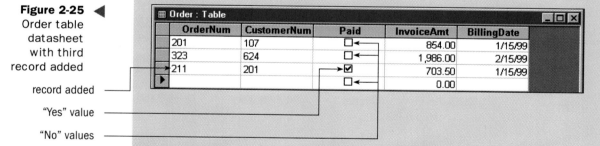

As you add records, Access places them at the end of the datasheet. If you switch to Design view then return to the datasheet or if you close the table then open the datasheet, Access will display the records in primary key sequence.

You have modified the Order table structure and added one record. Instead of typing the remaining records in the Order table, Barbara suggests that you copy them from a table that already exists in another database, and then paste them into the Order table.

Copying Records from Another Access Database

You can copy and paste records from a table in the same database or in a different database, but only if the tables have the same table structure. Barbara's Valle database in the Tutorial folder on your Student Disk has a table named Restaurant Order, which has the same table structure as the Order table. The records in the Restaurant Order table are the records Barbara wants you to copy into the Order table.

Other programs, such as Microsoft Word and Microsoft Excel, allow you to have two or more documents open at a time. However, you can have only one Access database open at a time. Therefore, you need to close the Restaurant database, open the Restaurant Order table in the Valle database, select and copy the table records, close the Valle database, reopen the Order table in the Restaurant database, and then paste the copied records.

To copy the records from the Restaurant Order table:

1. Click the **Close** button ⊠ on the Table window title bar to close the Order table, and then click the **Close** button ⊠ on the Database window title bar to close the Restaurant database.

2. Click the **Open Database** button 📂 on the Database toolbar. The Open dialog box opens.

3. If necessary, display the list of files on your Student Disk, and then open the **Tutorial** folder.

4. Open the file named **Valle**. The Database window opens, showing the tables for the Valle database.

   Notice that the Valle database contains two tables: the Restaurant Customer table and the Restaurant Order table. The Restaurant Order table contains the records you need to copy.

5. Click **Restaurant Order** in the Tables list box, and then click the **Open** button. The datasheet for the Restaurant Order table opens. See Figure 2-26. Note that this table contains a total of 102 records.

Figure 2-26 ◄
Datasheet for
the Valle
database's
Restaurant
Order table

click here to
select all records

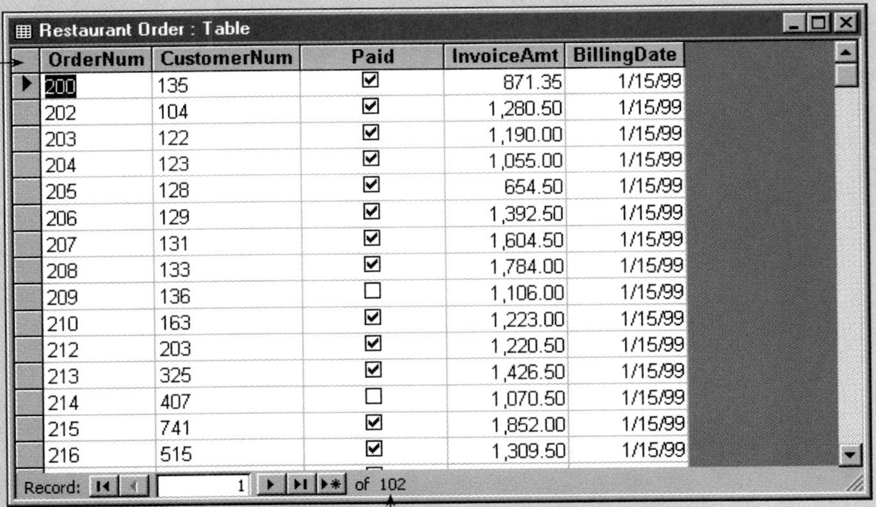

OrderNum	CustomerNum	Paid	InvoiceAmt	BillingDate
200	135	☑	871.35	1/15/99
202	104	☑	1,280.50	1/15/99
203	122	☑	1,190.00	1/15/99
204	123	☑	1,055.00	1/15/99
205	128	☑	654.50	1/15/99
206	129	☑	1,392.50	1/15/99
207	131	☑	1,604.50	1/15/99
208	133	☑	1,784.00	1/15/99
209	136	☐	1,106.00	1/15/99
210	163	☑	1,223.00	1/15/99
212	203	☑	1,220.50	1/15/99
213	325	☑	1,426.50	1/15/99
214	407	☐	1,070.50	1/15/99
215	741	☑	1,852.00	1/15/99
216	515	☑	1,309.50	1/15/99

Record: 1 of 102

total number of
records in the table

Barbara wants you to copy all the records in the Restaurant Order table. You can select all records by clicking the row selector for the field name row.

6. Click the **row selector** for the field name row (see Figure 2-26). All the records in the table are now highlighted, which means that Access has selected all of them.

7. Click the **Copy** button 📋 on the Table Datasheet toolbar. All the records are copied to the Clipboard.

8. Click the **Close** button ⊠ on the Table window title bar. A dialog box opens asking if you want to save the data you copied on the Clipboard.

9. Click the **Yes** button in the dialog box. The dialog box closes and then the table closes.

10. Click the **Close** button ☒ on the Database window title bar to close the Valle database.

To finish copying and pasting the records, you must open the Order table and paste the copied records into the table.

To paste the copied records into the Order table:

1. Click **File** on the menu bar, and then click **Restaurant** in the list of recently opened databases. The Database window opens, showing the tables for the Restaurant database.

2. In the Tables list box, click **Order** and then click the **Open** button. The datasheet for the Order table opens.

   You must paste the records at the end of the table.

3. Click the **row selector** for row four, which is the next row available for a new record.

4. Click the **Paste** button 📋 on the Table Datasheet toolbar. All the records are pasted from the Clipboard, and a dialog box appears, asking if you are sure you want to paste the records.

5. Click the **Yes** button. The pasted records remain highlighted. See Figure 2-27. Notice that the table now contains a total of 105 records—the three original records plus the 102 copied records.

Figure 2-27 ◀
Table after copying and pasting records

original records (3)

pasted records (102)

table now contains a total of 105 records

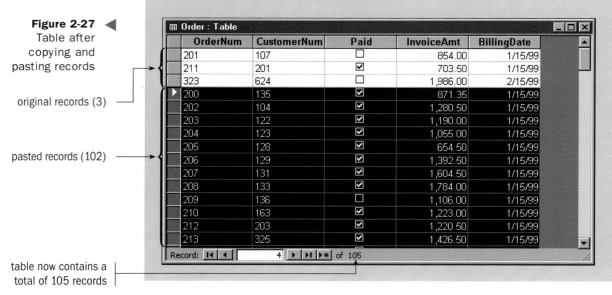

You've completed copying and pasting the records between the two tables. Now that you have all the records in the Order table, Barbara examines the records to make sure they are correct. She finds one record that she wants you to delete and another record that needs changes to its field values.

Updating a Database

Updating, or **maintaining**, a database is the process of adding, changing, and deleting records in database tables to keep them current and accurate. You've already added records to the Order table. Now Barbara wants you to delete and change records.

Deleting Records

To delete a record, you need to select the record in Datasheet view, and then delete it using the Delete Record button on the Table Datasheet toolbar or the Delete Record option on the shortcut menu.

REFERENCE window

DELETING A RECORD

- In the Table window in Datasheet view, click the row selector for the record you want to delete and then click the Delete Record button on the Table Datasheet toolbar (or right-click the row selector for the record, and then click Delete Record on the shortcut menu).
- In the dialog box asking you to confirm the deletion, click the Yes button.

Barbara asks you to delete the record whose OrderNum is 200 because this record was entered in error; it represents an order from an office customer, not a restaurant customer, and therefore does not belong in the Restaurant database. The fourth record in the table has an OrderNum value of 200. This is the record you need to delete.

To delete the record:

1. Right-click the **row selector** for row four. Access selects the fourth record and displays the shortcut menu. See Figure 2-28.

Figure 2-28 ◀
Deleting
a record

selected record ————

click to delete the
selected record

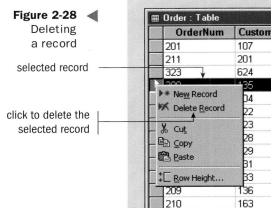

2. Click **Delete Record** on the shortcut menu. Access deletes the record and opens a dialog box asking you to confirm the deletion.

   TROUBLE? If you selected the wrong record for deletion, click the No button. Access ends the deletion process and redisplays the deleted record. Repeat Steps 1 and 2 to delete the correct record.

3. Click the **Yes** button to confirm the deletion and close the dialog box.

Barbara's final update to the Order table involves changes to field values in one of the records.

Changing Records

To change the field values in a record, you first must make the record the current record. Then you position the insertion point in the field value to make minor changes or select the field value to replace it entirely. In Tutorial 1, you used the mouse with the scroll bars and the navigation buttons to navigate through the records in a datasheet. You can also use keystroke combinations and the F2 key to navigate a datasheet and to select field values.

The **F2 key** is a toggle that you use to switch between navigation mode and editing mode:

- In **navigation mode**, Access selects an entire field value. If you type while you are in navigation mode, your typed entry replaces the highlighted field value.

- In **editing mode**, you can insert or delete characters in a field value based on the location of the insertion point.

The navigation mode and editing mode keystroke techniques are shown in Figure 2-29.

Figure 2-29 ◄
Navigation
mode and
editing mode
keystroke
techniques

Press	To Move the Selection in Navigation Mode	To Move the Insertion Point in Editing Mode
←	Left one field value at a time	Left one character at a time
→	Right one field value at a time	Right one character at a time
Home	Left to the first field value in the record	To the left of the first character in the field value
End	Right to the last field value in the record	To the right of the last character in the field value
↑ or ↓	Up or down one record at a time	Up or down one record at a time and switch to navigation mode
Tab or Enter	Right one field value at a time	Right one field value at a time and switch to navigation mode
Ctrl + Home	To the first field value in the first record	To the left of the first character in the field value
Ctrl + End	To the last field value in the last record	To the right of the last character in the field value

The record Barbara wants you to change has an OrderNum field value of 397. Some of the values were entered incorrectly for this record, and you need to enter the correct values.

To modify the record:

1. Make sure the OrderNum field value for the fourth record is still highlighted, indicating that the table is in navigation mode.

2. Press **Ctrl + End**. Access displays records from the end of the table and selects the last field value in the last record. This field value is for the BillingDate field.

3. Press the **Home** key. The first field value in the record is now selected. This field value is for the OrderNum field.

4. Press the ↑ key. The OrderNum field value for the previous record is selected. This is the record you need to change.

Barbara wants you to change these field values in the record: OrderNum to 398, CustomerNum to 165, Paid to "Yes" (checked), and InvoiceAmt to 1426.50. The BillingDate does not need to be changed.

5. Type **398**, press the **Tab** key, type **165**, press the **Tab** key, press the **spacebar** to insert a check mark in the Paid check box, press the **Tab** key, and then type **1426.5**. This completes the changes to the record.

6. Press the ↓ key to save the changes to the record and make the next record the current record. See Figure 2-30.

Figure 2-30 ◀
Table after changing field values in a record

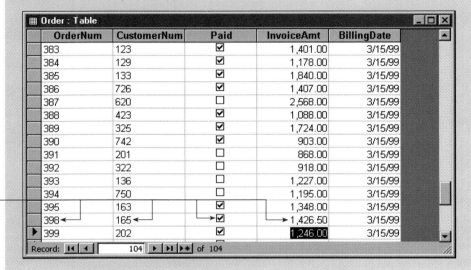

field values changed

You've completed all of Barbara's updates to the Order table. Barbara asks you to print just the first page of data from the Order table datasheet so that she can show the revised table structure to her staff members. After you print the page, you can exit Access.

To print the first page of Order table data, and then exit Access:

1. Click **File** on the menu bar, and then click **Print** to display the Print dialog box.

2. In the Print Range section, click the **Pages** option button, type **1** in the From text box, press the **Tab** key, and then type **1** in the To text box.

3. Click the **OK** button to print the first page of data.

   Now you can exit Access.

4. Click the **Close** button ⊠ on the Access window title bar to close the Order table and the Restaurant database and to exit Access.

Quick Check

1   What is the effect of deleting a field from a table structure?

2   How do you insert a field between existing fields in a table structure?

3   A field with the _____ data type can appear in the table datasheet as a check box.

4   Which property do you use to control the display appearance of a field value?

5   Why must you close an open database when you want to copy records to it from a table in another database?

6   What is the difference between navigation mode and editing mode?

Barbara and her staff members approve of the revised table structure for the Order table. They are confident that the table will allow them to easily track order data for Valle Coffee's restaurant customers.

Tutorial Assignments

Barbara needs a database to track the coffee products offered by Valle Coffee. She asks you to create the database by completing the following:

1. Make sure your Student Disk is in the disk drive, and then start Access.

2. In the initial Access dialog box, click the Blank Database option button, and then click the OK button. In the File New Database dialog box, select the TAssign folder on your Student Disk, and then enter the filename Valle Products for the database. Click the Create button to create the new database.

3. Create a table using the table design shown in Figure 2-31.

Figure 2-31 ◀

Field Name	Data Type	Description	Field Size	Other Properties
ProductCode	Text	primary key	4	
CoffeeCode	Text	foreign key	4	
Price	Currency	price for this product		Format: Fixed Decimal Places: 2
Decaf	Text	D if decaf, Null if regular	1	Default Value: D
BackOrdered	Yes/No	back-ordered from supplier?		

4. Specify ProductCode as the primary key, and then save the table as Product.

5. Add the product records shown in Figure 2-32 to the Product table.

Figure 2-32 ◀

ProductCode	CoffeeCode	Price	Decaf	BackOrdered
2316	JRUM	8.99		Yes
9754	HAZL	40.00	D	No
9309	COCO	9.99	D	No

6. Make the following changes to the structure of the Product table:
   a. Add a new field between the CoffeeCode and Price fields, using these properties:
   Field Name: WeightCode
   Data Type: Text
   Description: foreign key
   Field Size: 1
   b. Move the BackOrdered field so that it appears between the WeightCode and Price fields.
   c. Save the revised table structure.

7. Use the Product datasheet to update the database as follows:
   a. Enter these WeightCode values for the three records: A for ProductCode 2316, A for ProductCode 9309, and E for ProductCode 9754.

b. Add a record to the Product datasheet with these field values:

ProductCode:	9729
CoffeeCode:	COLS
WeightCode:	E
BackOrdered:	No
Price:	37.50
Decaf:	D

8. Barbara created a database with her name as the database name. The Coffee Product table in that database has the same format as the Product table you created. Copy all the records from the Coffee Product table in the Barbara database (located in the TAssign folder on your Student Disk) to the end of your Product table.

9. Close the Product table, and then reopen it so that the records are displayed in primary key order by ProductCode. Then delete the record with the ProductCode 2333 from the Product table.

10. Delete the BackOrdered field from the Product table structure.

11. Use the Access Help system to learn how to resize datasheet columns to fit the data, and then resize all columns in the datasheet for the Product table so that each column fits its data. Scroll the datasheet to make sure all field values are fully displayed. For any field values that are not fully displayed, make sure the field values are visible on the screen, and then resize the appropriate columns again.

12. Print the first page of data from the Product table datasheet, and then save and close the table.

13. Create a table named Weight based on the data shown in Figure 2-33.

Figure 2-33 ◀

WeightCode	Weight/Size
A	1 lb pkg
B	6 lb case
C	24 ct 1.5 oz pkg
D	44 ct 1.25 oz pkg
E	44 ct 1.5 oz pkg
F	88 ct 1.25 oz pkg
G	88 ct 1.5 oz pkg

a. Select the Datasheet View option in the New Table dialog box.
b. Enter the seven records shown in Figure 2-33. (Do *not* enter the field names at this point.)
c. Switch to Design view, supply the table name, and then answer No if asked if you want to create a primary key.
d. Type the following field names and set the following properties:
   WeightCode
Description:	primary key
Field Size:	1

   Weight/Size
Description:	weight in pounds or size in packages (number and weight) per case
Field Size:	17
e. Specify the primary key, save the table structure changes, and then switch back to Datasheet view. If you receive any warning messages, answer Yes to continue.

f. Resize both datasheet columns to fit the data (use Access Help to learn how to resize datasheet columns, if necessary); then save, print, and close the datasheet.

14. Create a table named Coffee using the Import Table Wizard. The table you need to import is named Coffee.dbf and is located in the TAssign folder on your Student Disk. This table has a dBASE 5 file type. (You'll need to change the entry in the Files of type list box to display the file in the list.) After importing the table, complete the following:

a. Change all field names to use the Valle Coffee convention of uppercase and lowercase letters, and then enter the following Description property values:
CoffeeCode: primary key
Decaf: Is decaf available for this coffee?

b. Change the Format property of the Decaf field to Yes/No.

c. Specify the primary key, and then save the table structure changes.

d. Switch to Datasheet view, and then resize all columns in the datasheet to fit the data. (Use Access Help to learn how to resize datasheet columns, if necessary.) Be sure to scroll through the table to make sure that all field values are fully displayed.

e. Save, print, and then close the datasheet. Close the Valle Products database.

Case Problems

1. Ashbrook Mall Information Desk Sam Bullard, the director of the Mall Operations Office at Ashbrook Mall, uses the MallJobs database to maintain information about current job openings at stores in the mall. Sam asks you to help him maintain the database by completing the following:

1. Make sure your Student Disk is in the disk drive.

2. Start Access and open the MallJobs database located in the Cases folder on your Student Disk.

3. Create a table using the table design shown in Figure 2-34.

Figure 2-34 ◄

Field Name	Data Type	Description	Field Size
Job	Text	primary key	5
Store	Text	foreign key	3
Hours/Week	Text		20
Position	Text		35
ExperienceReq	Yes/No		

4. Specify Job as the primary key, and then save the table as Job.

5. Add the job records shown in Figure 2-35 to the Job table.

Figure 2-35 ◄

Job	Store	Hours/Week	Position	ExperienceReq
10037	WT	negotiable	Salesclerk	No
10053	BR	14-24	Server Assistant	No
10022	JP	35-45	Assistant Manager	Yes

6. Sam created a database named Openings that contains a table with job data named Current Jobs. The Job table you created has the same format as the Current Jobs table. Copy all the records from the Current Jobs table in the Openings database (located in the Cases folder on your Student Disk) to the end of your Job table.

7. Modify the structure of the Job table by completing the following:
   a. Delete the ExperienceReq field.
   b. Move the Hours/Week field so that it follows the Position field.

8. Use the Access Help system to learn how to resize datasheet columns to fit the data, and then switch to Datasheet view and resize all columns in the datasheet for the Job table.

9. Use the Job datasheet to update the database as follows:
   a. For Job 10046, change the Position value to Clerk, and change the Hours/Week value to 20-30.
   b. Add a record to the Job datasheet with the following field values:
      Job: 10034
      Store: JP
      Position: Salesclerk
      Hours/Week: negotiable
   c. Delete the record for Job 10029.

10. Switch to Design view, and then switch back to Datasheet view so that the records are displayed in primary key sequence by Job.

11. Print the Job table datasheet, and then save and close the table. Close the MallJobs database.

2. Professional Litigation User Services Raj Jawahir is responsible for tracking the daily payments received from PLUS clients. You'll help him maintain the Payments database by completing the following:

1. Make sure your Student Disk is in the disk drive.

2. Start Access and open the Payments database located in the Cases folder on your Student Disk.

3. Create a table named Payment using the table design shown in Figure 2-36.

Figure 2-36 ◀

Field Name	Data Type	Description	Field Size	Other Properties
Payment#	Text	primary key	5	
Firm#	Text	foreign key	4	
DatePaid	Date/Time			Format: Medium Date
AmtPaid	Currency			Format: Standard
				Decimal Places: 2
				Default Value: 0

4. Add the payment records shown in Figure 2-37 to the Payment table.

Figure 2-37 ◀

Payment#	Firm#	DatePaid	AmtPaid
10031	1147	6/3/99	2435.00
10002	1100	6/1/99	1300.00
10015	1142	6/1/99	2000.00

5. Modify the structure of the Payment table by completing the following:
   a. Add a new field between the Payment# and Firm# fields, using these properties:
      Field Name: Deposit#
      Data Type: Text
      Field Size: 3
   b. Move the DatePaid field so that it follows the AmtPaid field.

6. Use the Payment datasheet to update the database as follows:
   a. Enter these Deposit# values for the three records: 100 for Payment# 10002, 101 for Payment# 10015, and 103 for Payment# 10031.
   b. Add a record to the Payment datasheet with these field values:
   Payment#: 10105
   Deposit#: 117
   Firm#: 1103
   AmtPaid: 2,500.00
   DatePaid: 6/20/99

7. Raj created a database named PlusPays that contains recent payments in the Payment Records table. The Payment table you created has the same format as the Payment Records table. Copy all the records from the Payment Records table in the PlusPays database (located in the Cases folder on your Student Disk) to the end of your Payment table.

8. Use the Access Help system to learn how to resize datasheet columns to fit the data, and then resize all columns in the datasheet for the Payment table.

9. For Payment# 10002, change the AmtPaid value to 1100.00.

10. Delete the record for Payment# 10101.

11. Print the first page of data from the Payment table datasheet, and then save and close the table. Close the Payments database.

3. Best Friends Noah and Sheila Warnick continue to track information about participants in the Walk-A-Thons held to benefit Best Friends. Help them maintain the Walks database by completing the following:

1. Make sure your Student Disk is in the disk drive.

2. Start Access and open the Walks database located in the Cases folder on your Student Disk.

3. Create a table named Pledge using the Import Table Wizard. The table you need to import is named Pledge.dbf and is located in the Cases folder on your Student Disk. This table has a Microsoft FoxPro file type. (You'll need to change the entry in the Files of type list box to display the file in the list. Make sure you choose the Microsoft FoxPro file type, not the Microsoft FoxPro 3.0 file type.) After importing the table, complete the following:
   a. Change all field names to use uppercase and lowercase letters, as appropriate, and then enter the following Description property values:
   PledgeNo: primary key
   WalkerID: foreign key
   PerMile: amount pledged per mile
   b. Specify the primary key, and then save the table structure changes.
   c. Switch to Datasheet view, and then resize all columns in the datasheet to fit the data. (Use Access Help to learn how to resize datasheet columns, if necessary.)

4. Modify the structure of the Pledge table by completing the following:
   a. Add a new field between the PaidAmt and PerMile fields, using these properties:
   Field Name: DatePaid
   Data Type: Date/Time
   Format: Medium Date
   b. Change the Data Type of both the PledgeAmt field and the PaidAmt field to Currency. For each of these fields, choose the Fixed format.

5. Use the Pledge datasheet to update the database as follows:
   a. Enter these DatePaid values for the five records: 9/15/99 for PledgeNo 1, 9/1/99 for PledgeNo 2, 8/27/99 for PledgeNo 3, 9/20/99 for PledgeNo 4, and 8/30/99 for PledgeNo 5. Resize the DataPaid column to fit the data.
   b. Add a record to the Pledge datasheet with these field values:
      PledgeNo: 6
      Pledger: Fernando Carazana
      WalkerID: 138
      PledgeAmt: 25
      PaidAmt: 25
      DatePaid: 9/18/99
      PerMile: 0
   c. Enter the value 183 in the WalkerID field for PledgeNo 1.
   d. Change both the PledgeAmt value and the PaidAmt value for PledgeNo 3 to 10.00.
   e. Change the WalkerID value for PledgeNo 5 to 187.

6. Print the Pledge table datasheet, and then save and close the table. Close the Walks database.

4. Lopez Lexus Dealerships Maria and Hector Lopez use the Lexus database to track the car inventory in the chain of Lexus dealerships they own. You'll help them maintain the Lexus database by completing the following:

1. Make sure your Student Disk is in the disk drive.

2. Start Access and open the Lexus database located in the Cases folder on your Student Disk.

3. Use the Import Spreadsheet Wizard to create a new table named Locations. The data you need to import is contained in the Lopez workbook, which is a Microsoft Excel file located in the Cases folder on your Student Disk.
   a. Select the Import Table option in the New Table dialog box.
   b. Change the entry in the Files of type list box to display the list of Excel workbook files in the Cases folder.
   c. Select the Lopez file and then click the Import button.
   d. In the Import Spreadsheet Wizard dialog boxes, choose the option for using column headings as field names; select the option for choosing your own primary key and specify LocationCode as the primary key; and enter the table name (Locations). Otherwise, accept the wizard's choices for all other options for the imported data.

4. Use the Access Help system to learn how to resize datasheet columns to fit the data, and then open the Locations table and resize all columns in the datasheet.

5. Modify the structure of the Locations table by completing the following:
   a. For the LocationCode field, enter a Description property of "primary key," change the Field Size to 2, and change the Required property to Yes.
   b. For the LocationName field, change the Field Size to 20.
   c. For the ManagerName field, change the Field Size to 30.
   d. Save the table. If you receive any warning messages about lost data or integrity rules, click the Yes button.

6. Use the Locations datasheet to update the database as follows:
   a. For LocationCode A2, change the ManagerName value to Curran, Leo.
   b. Add a record to the Locations datasheet with these field values:

      LocationCode: H2
      LocationName: Houston
      ManagerName: Cohen, Sandra

   c. Delete the record for LocationCode L2.

7. Print the Locations table datasheet, and then close the table and the Lexus database.

Querying a Database

Retrieving Information About Restaurant Customers and Their Orders

In this tutorial you will:

- Learn how to use the Query window in Design view

- Create, run, and save queries

- Define a relationship between two tables

- Sort data in a query

- Filter data in a query

- Specify an exact match condition in a query

- Change a datasheet's appearance

- Use a comparison operator to match a range of values

- Use the And and Or logical operators

- Perform calculations in a query using calculated fields, aggregate functions, and record group calculations

CASE

Valle Coffee

At a recent company meeting, Leonard Valle and other Valle Coffee employees discussed the importance of regularly monitoring the business activity of the company's restaurant customers. For example, Kim Carpenter and her marketing staff track customer activity to develop new strategies for promoting Valle Coffee products. Barbara Hennessey and her office staff need to track information about all the orders for which bills were sent out on a specific date so that they can determine whether the bills have been paid. In addition, Leonard is interested in analyzing the payment history of restaurant customers to determine which customers pay their invoices in a timely manner, which customers have higher invoice amounts, and so on. All of these informational needs can be satisfied by queries that retrieve information from the Restaurant database.

In this session you will use the Query window in Design view to create, run, and save queries; define a one-to-many relationship between two tables; sort data with a toolbar button and in Design view; and filter data in a query datasheet.

Introduction to Queries

As you learned in Tutorial 1, a query is a question you ask about data stored in a database. For example, Kim might create a query to find records in the Customer table for only those customers in a specific state. When you create a query, you tell Access which fields you need and what criteria Access should use to select the records.

Access provides powerful query capabilities that allow you to:

- display selected fields and records from a table

- sort records

- perform calculations

- generate data for forms, reports, and other queries

- update data in the tables in a database

- find and display data from two or more tables

Most questions about data are generalized queries in which you specify the fields and records you want Access to select. These common requests for information, such as "Which customers have unpaid bills?" or "Which type of coffee sells best in Ohio?" are called **select queries**. The answer to a select query is returned in the form of a datasheet.

More specialized, technical queries, such as finding duplicate records in a table, are best formulated through a Query Wizard. A Query Wizard prompts you for information through a set of questions and then creates the appropriate query based on your answers. In Tutorial 1, you used the Simple Query Wizard to display only some of the fields in the Customer table; Access provides other Query Wizards for more complex queries. For common, informational queries, it is easier for you to design your own query rather than use a Query Wizard.

Kim wants you to create a query to display the customer number, customer name, city, owner name, and first contact information for each record in the Customer table. She needs this information for a market analysis her staff is completing on Valle Coffee's restaurant customers. You'll open the Query window to create the query for Kim.

The Query Window

You use the Query window in Design view to create a query. In Design view you specify the data you want to view by constructing a query by example. Using **query by example (QBE)**, you give Access an example of the information you are requesting. Access then retrieves the information that precisely matches your example.

For Kim's query, you need to display data from the Customer table. You'll begin by starting Access, opening the Restaurant database, and displaying the Query window in Design view.

To start Access, open the Restaurant database, and open the Query window in Design view:

1. Place your Student Disk in the appropriate disk drive.

2. Start Access and open the Restaurant database located in the Tutorial folder on your Student Disk. The Restaurant database is displayed in the Access window.

3. Click the **Queries** tab in the Database window, and then click the **New** button. The New Query dialog box opens. See Figure 3-1.

Figure 3-1 ◀
New Query
dialog box

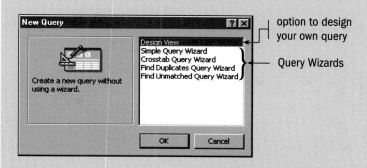

option to design
your own query

Query Wizards

You'll design your own query instead of using a Query Wizard.

4. If necessary, click **Design View** in the list box.

5. Click the **OK** button. Access opens the Show Table dialog box on top of the Query window. Notice that the title bar of the window shows that you are creating a select query.

The query you are creating will retrieve data from the Customer table, so you need to add this table to the Select Query window.

6. Click **Customer** in the Tables list box (if necessary), click the **Add** button, and then click the **Close** button. Access places the Customer table field list in the Select Query window and closes the dialog box.

To display more of the fields you'll be using for creating queries, you'll maximize the Select Query window.

7. Click the **Maximize** button 🔲 on the Select Query window title bar. See Figure 3-2.

Query Type button
shows select query   Run button

Figure 3-2 ◀
Select Query
window in
Design view

View button for
Datasheet view

field list

design grid

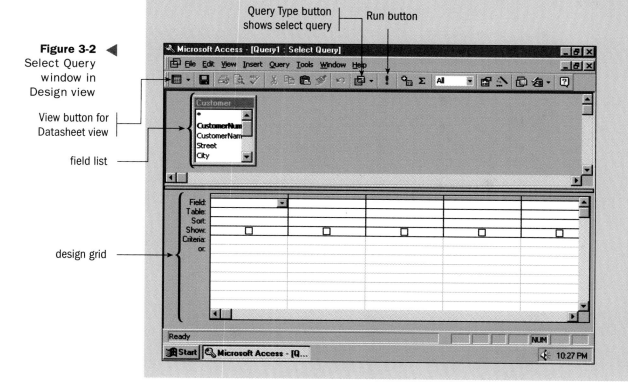

In Design view, the Select Query window contains the standard title bar, menu bar, toolbar, and status bar. On the toolbar, the Query Type button shows a select query; the icon on this button changes according to the type of query you are creating. The title bar on the Select Query window displays the query type, Select Query, and the default query name, Query1. You'll change the default query name to a more meaningful one later when you save the query.

The Select Query window in Design view contains a field list and the design grid. The **field list**, which appears in the upper-left area of the window, contains the fields for the table you are querying. The table name appears at the top of the list box, and the fields are listed in the order in which they appear in the table.

In the **design grid**, you include the fields and record selection criteria for the information you want to see. Each column in the design grid contains specifications about a field you will use in the query. You can choose a single field for your query by dragging its name from the field list to the design grid in the lower portion of the window. Alternatively, you can double-click a field name to place it in the next available column in the design grid.

When you are constructing a query, you can see the query results at any time by clicking the View button or the Run button on the Query Design toolbar. In response, Access displays the datasheet, which contains the set of fields and records that result from answering, or **running**, the query. The order of the fields in the datasheet is the same as the order of the fields in the design grid. Although the datasheet looks just like a table datasheet and appears in Datasheet view, a query datasheet is temporary and its contents are based on the criteria you establish in the design grid. In contrast, a table datasheet shows the permanent data in a table. However, you can update data while viewing a query datasheet, just as you can when working in a table datasheet or a form.

If the query you are creating includes all the fields from the specified table, you could use one of the following three methods to transfer all the fields from the field list to the design grid:

- Click and drag each field individually from the field list to the design grid. Use this method if you want the fields in your query to appear in an order that is different from the order in the field list.

- Double-click the asterisk in the field list. Access places the table name followed by a period and an asterisk (as in "Customer.*") in the design grid. This signifies that the order of the fields will be the same in the query as it is in the field list. Use this method if the query does not need to be sorted or to have conditions for the records you want to select. The advantage of using this method is that you do not need to change the query if you add or delete fields from the underlying table structure. They will all appear automatically in the query.

- Double-click the field list title bar to highlight all the fields, and then click and drag one of the highlighted fields to the design grid. Access places each field in a separate column and arranges the fields in the order in which they appear in the field list. Use this method rather than the previous one if your query needs to be sorted or to include record selection criteria.

Now you'll create and run Kim's query to display selected fields from the Customer table.

Creating and Running a Query

A table datasheet displays all the fields in the table, in the same order as they appear in the table. In contrast, a query datasheet can display selected fields from a table, and the order of the fields can be different from that of the table.

Kim wants the CustomerNum, CustomerName, City, OwnerName, and FirstContact fields to appear in the query results. You'll add each of these fields to the design grid.

To select the fields for the query, and then run the query:

1. Drag **CustomerNum** from the Customer field list to the design grid's first column Field text box, and then release the mouse button. See Figure 3-3.

Figure 3-3 ◀
Field added to
the design grid

drag field from here

release mouse
button here

indicates that the
field will appear
in the datasheet

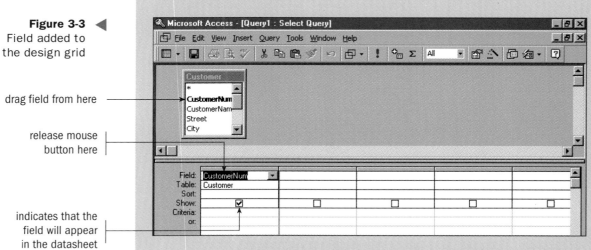

In the design grid's first column, the field name CustomerNum appears in the Field text box, the table name Customer appears in the Table text box, and the check mark in the Show check box indicates that the field will be displayed in the datasheet when you run the query. There are times when you might choose not to display a field and its values in the query results. For example, if you are creating a query to show all the customers located in Michigan, and you assign the name "Customers in Michigan" to the query, you would not need to include the State field value for each record in the query results. Even if you choose not to include a field in the display of the query results, you can still use the field as part of the query to select specific records or to specify a particular sequence for the records in the datasheet.

2. Double-click **CustomerName** in the Customer field list. Access adds this field to the second column of the design grid.

3. Scrolling the Customer field list as necessary, repeat Step 2 for the **City**, **OwnerName**, and **FirstContact** fields to add these fields to the design grid in that order.

Having selected the fields for Kim's query, you can now run the query.

4. Click the **Run** button � on the Query Design toolbar. Access runs the query and displays the results in Datasheet view. See Figure 3-4.

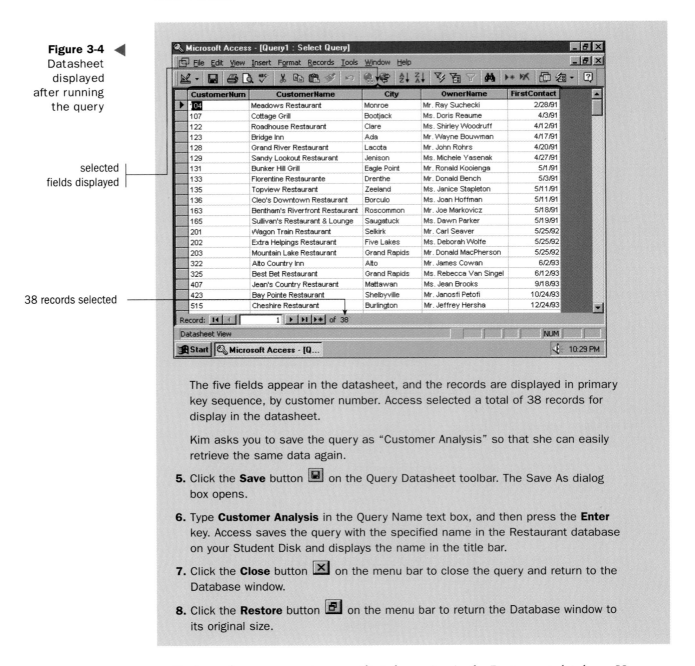

Figure 3-4
Datasheet
displayed
after running
the query

selected
fields displayed

38 records selected

The five fields appear in the datasheet, and the records are displayed in primary key sequence, by customer number. Access selected a total of 38 records for display in the datasheet.

Kim asks you to save the query as "Customer Analysis" so that she can easily retrieve the same data again.

5. Click the **Save** button 🖬 on the Query Datasheet toolbar. The Save As dialog box opens.

6. Type **Customer Analysis** in the Query Name text box, and then press the **Enter** key. Access saves the query with the specified name in the Restaurant database on your Student Disk and displays the name in the title bar.

7. Click the **Close** button ⊠ on the menu bar to close the query and return to the Database window.

8. Click the **Restore** button 🖻 on the menu bar to return the Database window to its original size.

Barbara also wants to view specific information in the Restaurant database. However, she needs to see data from both the Customer table and the Order table at the same time. To accomplish this, you need to define a relationship between the two tables.

Defining Table Relationships

One of the most powerful features of a relational database management system is its ability to define relationships between tables. You use a common field to relate one table to another. The process of relating tables is often called performing a **join**. When you join tables that have a common field, you can extract data from them as if they were one larger table. For example, you can join the Customer and Order tables by using the CustomerNum field in both tables as the common field. You then can use a query, form, or report to extract selected data from each table, even though the data is contained in two separate tables, as shown in Figure 3-5. In the Orders query shown in Figure 3-5, the OrderNum, Paid, and InvoiceAmt columns are fields from the Order table; and the CustomerName and State columns are fields from the Customer table. The joining of records is based on the common field of CustomerNum. The Customer and Order tables have a type of relationship called a one-to-many relationship.

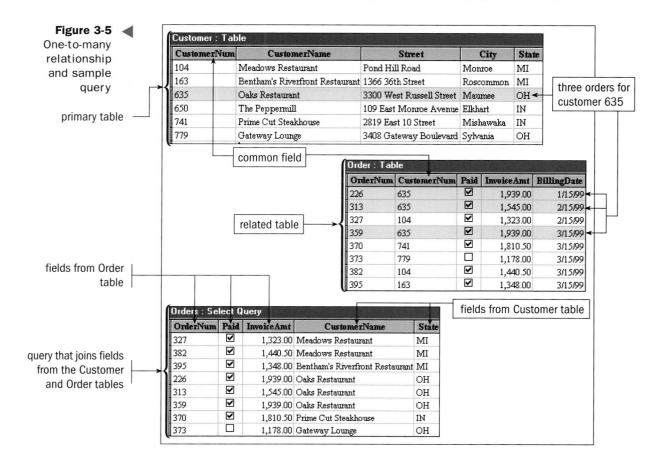

Figure 3-5 ◀
One-to-many
relationship
and sample
query

primary table —

fields from Order
table

query that joins fields
from the Customer
and Order tables

One-to-Many Relationships

A **one-to-many relationship** exists between two tables when one record in the first table matches zero, one, or many records in the second table, and when one record in the second table matches exactly one record in the first table. For example, as shown in Figure 3-5, customer 635 has three orders, customer 650 has zero orders, customers 163, 741, and 779 each have one order, and customer 104 has two orders. Every order has a single matching customer.

Access refers to the two tables that form a relationship as the primary table and the related table. The **primary table** is the "one" table in a one-to-many relationship; in Figure 3-5, the Customer table is the primary table because there is only one customer for each order. The **related table** is the "many" table; in Figure 3-5, the Order table is the related table because there can be many orders for each customer.

Because related data is stored in two tables, inconsistencies between the tables can occur. Consider the following scenarios:

- Barbara adds an order to the Order table for customer 107, Cottage Grill. This order does not have a matching record in the Customer table. The data is inconsistent, and the order record is considered to be an **orphaned** record.

- Barbara changes Oaks Restaurant from customer number 635 to 997 in the Customer table. Three orphaned records for customer 635 now exist in the Order table, and the database is inconsistent.

- Barbara deletes the record for Meadows Restaurant, customer 104, in the Customer table because this customer is no longer a Valle Coffee customer. The database is again inconsistent; two records for customer 104 in the Order table have no matching record in the Customer table.

You can avoid these problems by specifying referential integrity between tables when you define their relationships.

Referential Integrity

Referential integrity is a set of rules that Access enforces to maintain consistency between related tables when you update data in a database. Specifically, the referential integrity rules are as follows:

- When you add a record to a related table, a matching record must already exist in the primary table.

- If you attempt to change the value of the primary key in the primary table, Access prevents this change if matching records exist in a related table. However, if you choose the **cascade updates** option, Access permits the change in value to the primary key and changes the appropriate foreign key values in the related table.

- When you delete a record in the primary table, Access prevents the deletion if matching records exist in a related table. However, if you choose the **cascade deletes** option, Access deletes the record in the primary table and all records in related tables that have matching foreign key values.

Now you'll define a one-to-many relationship between the Customer and Order tables so that you can use fields from both tables to create a query that will retrieve the information Barbara wants.

Defining a Relationship Between Two Tables

When two tables have a common field, you can define a relationship between them in the Relationships window. The **Relationships window** illustrates the relationships among a database's tables. In this window you can view or change existing relationships, define new relationships between tables, and rearrange the layout of the tables.

You need to open the Relationships window and define the relationship between the Customer and Order tables. You'll define a one-to-many relationship between the two tables, with Customer as the primary table and Order as the related table, and with CustomerNum as the common field (the primary key in the Customer table and a foreign key in the Order table).

To define a one-to-many relationship between the two tables:

1. Click the **Relationships** button ⊞ on the Database toolbar. Access displays the Show Table dialog box on top of the Relationships window. See Figure 3-6.

Figure 3-6 ◀
Show Table
dialog box

add both tables

Relationships window

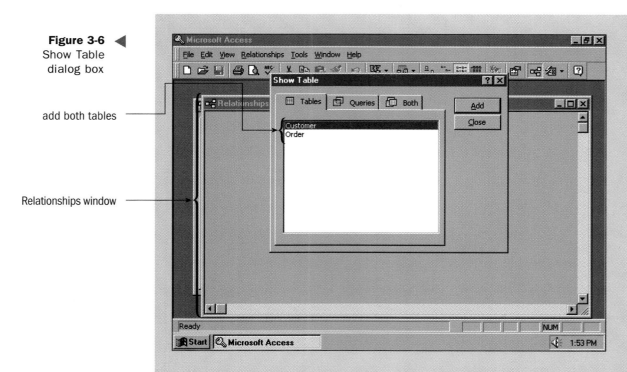

Each table participating in a relationship must be added to the Relationships window.

2. Click **Customer** (if necessary) and then click the **Add** button. The Customer table is added to the Relationships window.

3. Click **Order** and then click the **Add** button. The Order table is added to the Relationships window.

4. Click the **Close** button in the Show Table dialog box. Access closes the dialog box and reveals the entire Relationships window.

   To form the relationship between the two tables, you drag the common field of CustomerNum from the primary table to the related table. Access then opens the Relationships dialog box in which you select the relationship options for the two tables.

5. Click **CustomerNum** in the Customer table list, and drag it to **CustomerNum** in the Order table list. When you release the mouse button, Access opens the Relationships dialog box. See Figure 3-7.

Figure 3-7 ◀
Relationships
dialog box

primary table

common field

referential
integrity option

cascade options

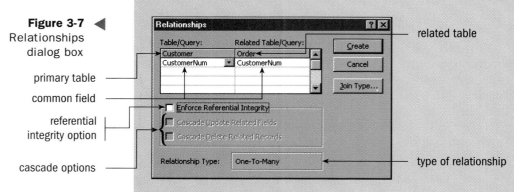

related table

type of relationship

The primary table, related table, and common field appear at the top of the dialog box. The type of relationship, one-to-many, appears at the bottom of the dialog box. When you click the Enforce Referential Integrity check box, the two cascade options become available. With the Cascade Update Related Fields option,

Access will change the appropriate foreign key values in the related table when you change a primary key value in the primary table. With the Cascade Delete Related Records option, when you delete a record in the primary table, Access will delete all records in the related table that have a matching foreign key value.

6. Click the **Enforce Referential Integrity** check box, click the **Cascade Update Related Fields** check box, and then click the **Cascade Delete Related Records** check box. You have now selected all the necessary relationship options.

7. Click the **Create** button to define the one-to-many relationship between the two tables and close the dialog box. The completed relationship appears in the Relationships window. See Figure 3-8.

Figure 3-8
Defined
relationship
in the
Relationships
window

"one" side of
the relationship

join line

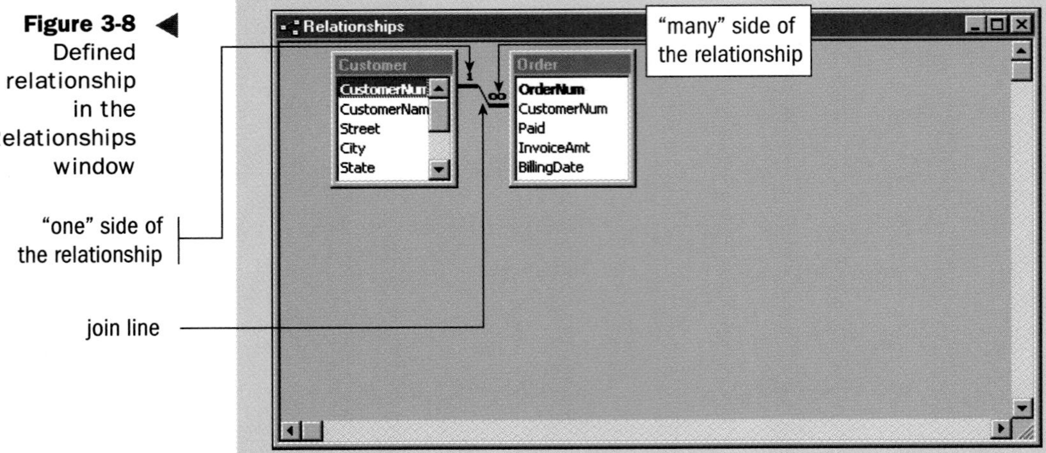

The *join line* connects the CustomerNum fields, which are common to the two tables. The common field joins the two tables, which have a one-to-many relationship. The join line is thick at both ends; this signifies that you have chosen the option to enforce referential integrity. If you do not select this option, the join line is thin at both ends. The "one" side of the relationship has the digit 1 at its end, and the "many" side of the relationship has the infinity symbol ∞ at its end. The two tables are still separate tables, but you can use the data in them as if they were one table.

8. Click the **Save** button 🖫 on the Relationship toolbar to save the layout in the Relationships window.

9. Click the **Close** button ☒ on the Relationships window title bar. Access closes the Relationships window and returns you to the Database window.

Now that you have joined the Customer and Order tables, you can create a query to produce the information Barbara wants. As part of her tracking of payments received from restaurant customers, Barbara needs a query that displays the CustomerName, City, and State fields from the Customer table and the BillingDate, InvoiceAmt, and Paid fields from the Order table.

To create, run, and save the query using the Customer and Order tables:

1. From the Queries tab in the Database window, click the **New** button to open the New Query dialog box, click **Design View** in the dialog box, and then click the **OK** button. Access opens the Show Table dialog box on top of the Query window in Design view.

You need to add both tables to the Query window.

2. Click **Customer** in the Tables list box (if necessary), click the **Add** button, click **Order**, click the **Add** button, and then click the **Close** button. Access places the

Customer and Order field lists in the Query window and closes the Show Table dialog box. Note that the one-to-many relationship that exists between the two tables is shown in the Query window.

You need to place the CustomerName, City, and State fields from the Customer field list into the design grid, and then place the BillingDate, InvoiceAmt, and Paid fields from the Order field list into the design grid.

3. Double-click **CustomerName** in the Customer field list. Access places CustomerName in the design grid's first column Field text box.

4. Repeat Step 3 to add the **City** and **State** fields from the Customer table, and then add the **BillingDate**, **InvoiceAmt**, and **Paid** fields (in that order) from the Order table, so that these fields are placed in the second through sixth columns of the design grid.

The query specifications are complete, so you can now run the query.

5. Click the **Run** button 🗒 on the Query Design toolbar. Access runs the query and displays the results in the datasheet.

6. Click the **Maximize** button ▢ on the Query window. See Figure 3-9.

Figure 3-9 ◀
Datasheet for
the query
based on the
Customer and
Order tables

fields from the
Customer table

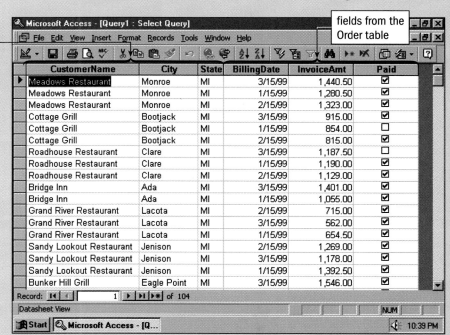

Only the six selected fields from the Customer and Order tables appear in the datasheet. The records are displayed in order according to the values in the primary key field, CustomerNum, even though this field is not included in the query datasheet.

Barbara plans on tracking the data retrieved by the query frequently, so she asks you to save the query as "Customer Orders."

7. Click the **Save** button 🖫 on the Query Datasheet toolbar. The Save As dialog box opens.

8. Type **Customer Orders** in the Query Name text box, and then press the **Enter** key. Access saves the query with the specified name and displays the name in the Query window title bar.

Barbara decides she wants the records displayed in alphabetical order by customer name. Because your query displays data in order by the field value of CustomerNum, the primary key for the Customer table, you need to sort the records by CustomerName to display the data in the order Barbara wants.

Sorting Data in a Query

Sorting is the process of rearranging records in a specified order or sequence. Often you need to sort data before displaying or printing it to meet a specific request. For example, Barbara might want to review order information arranged by the Paid field because she is interested in which orders are still unpaid. On the other hand, Leonard might want to view order information arranged by the InvoiceAmt totals for each customer because he tracks company sales.

When you sort data in a database, Access does not change the sequence of the records in the underlying tables. Only the records in the query datasheet are rearranged according to your specifications.

To sort records, you must select the **sort key**, which is the field used to determine the order of records in the datasheet. In this case, Barbara wants the data sorted by the customer name, so you need to specify the CustomerName field as the sort key. Sort keys can be text, number, date/time, currency, AutoNumber, or yes/no fields, but not memo, OLE object, or hyperlink fields. You sort records in either ascending (increasing) or descending (decreasing) order. Figure 3-10 shows the results of each type of sort for different data types.

Figure 3-10 ◀
Sorting results
for different
data types

Data Type	Ascending Sort Results	Descending Sort Results
Text	A to Z	Z to A
Number	lowest to highest numeric value	highest to lowest numeric value
Date/Time	oldest to most recent date	most recent to oldest date
Currency	lowest to highest numeric value	highest to lowest numeric value
AutoNumber	lowest to highest numeric value	highest to lowest numeric value
Yes/No	yes (check mark in check box) then no values	no then yes values

Access provides several methods for sorting data in a table or query datasheet and in a form. One method, clicking the toolbar sort buttons, lets you quickly sort the displayed records.

Using a Toolbar Button to Sort Data

The **Sort Ascending** and **Sort Descending** buttons on the toolbar allow you to sort records immediately, based on the selected field. First you select the column on which you want to base the sort, and then click the appropriate sort button on the toolbar to rearrange the records in either ascending or descending order. Unless you save the datasheet or form after you've sorted the records, the rearrangement of records is temporary.

Recall that in Tutorial 1 you used the Sort Ascending button to sort query results by the State field. You'll use this same button to sort the Customer Orders query results by the CustomerName field.

To sort the records using a toolbar sort button:

1. Click any visible CustomerName field value to establish this field as the current field.

2. Click the **Sort Ascending** button on the Query Datasheet toolbar. Access rearranges the records in ascending order by customer name. See Figure 3-11.

Figure 3-11
Sorting records on a single field in a datasheet

Sort Ascending button

Sort Descending button

records sorted in ascending order by CustomerName

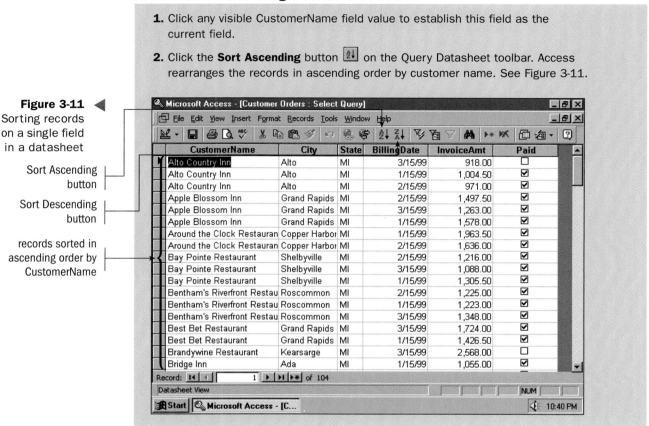

After viewing the query results, Barbara decides that she'd prefer the records to be arranged by the value in the Paid field so that she can determine more easily which invoices have been paid. She wants to view all the unpaid invoices before the paid invoices (descending order for the Paid field, which is a yes/no field); plus, she wants to display the records within each group in decreasing value of the InvoiceAmt field. To do this you need to sort using two fields.

Sorting Multiple Fields in Design View

Sort keys can be unique or nonunique. A sort key is **unique** if the value of the sort key field for each record is different. The CustomerNum field in the Customer table is an example of a unique sort key because each customer record has a different value in this field. A sort key is **nonunique** if more than one record can have the same value for the sort key field. The Paid field in the Order table is a nonunique sort key because more than one record has the same Paid value.

When the sort key is nonunique, records with the same sort key value are grouped together, but they are not in a specific order within the group. To arrange these grouped records in a specific order, you can specify a **secondary sort key**, which is a second sort key field. The first sort key field is called the **primary sort key**. Note that the primary sort key is not the same as a table's primary key field. A table has at most one primary key, which must be unique, whereas any field in a table can serve as a primary sort key.

Access lets you select up to 10 different sort keys. When you use the toolbar sort buttons, the sort key fields must be in adjacent columns in the datasheet. You highlight the columns, and Access sorts first by the first column and then by each other highlighted column in order from left to right.

Barbara wants the records sorted first by the Paid field and then by the InvoiceAmt field. Although the two fields are adjacent, they are in the wrong order. If you used a toolbar sort button, the InvoiceAmt field would be the primary sort key instead of the Paid field. When you have two or more nonadjacent sort keys or when the fields to be used for sorting are in the wrong order, you must specify the sort keys in the Query window in Design view. Access first uses the sort key that is leftmost in the design grid. Therefore, you must arrange the fields you want to sort from left to right in the design grid with the primary sort key being the leftmost sort key field.

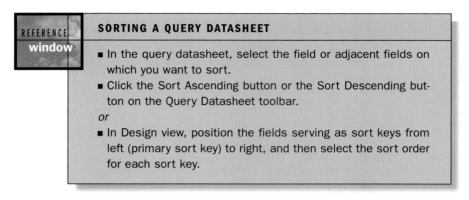

REFERENCE window

SORTING A QUERY DATASHEET

- In the query datasheet, select the field or adjacent fields on which you want to sort.
- Click the Sort Ascending button or the Sort Descending button on the Query Datasheet toolbar.

or

- In Design view, position the fields serving as sort keys from left (primary sort key) to right, and then select the sort order for each sort key.

To achieve the results Barbara wants, you need to switch to Design view, move the InvoiceAmt field to the right of the Paid field, and then specify the sort order for the two fields.

To select the two sort keys in Design view:

1. Click the **View** button for Design view ⊞ on the Query Datasheet toolbar. Access closes the window and opens the query in Design view.

   First, you'll move the InvoiceAmt field to the right of the Paid field.

2. If necessary, click the right arrow in the design grid's horizontal scroll bar to scroll to the right until both the InvoiceAmt and Paid fields are visible.

3. Position the pointer above the InvoiceAmt field name until the pointer changes to ↓ , and then click to select the field. See Figure 3-12.

field selector

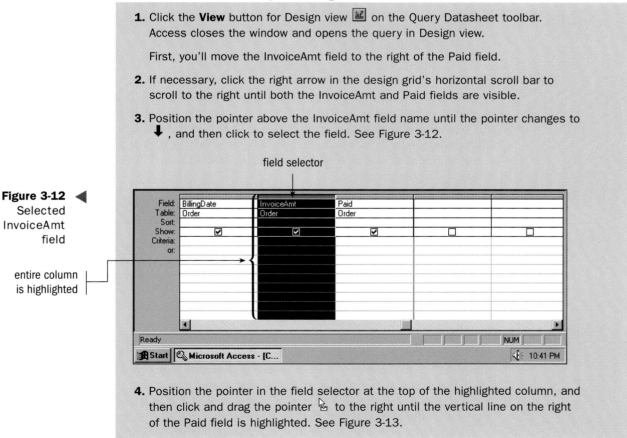

Figure 3-12 ◄
Selected
InvoiceAmt
field

entire column
is highlighted

4. Position the pointer in the field selector at the top of the highlighted column, and then click and drag the pointer ₖ to the right until the vertical line on the right of the Paid field is highlighted. See Figure 3-13.

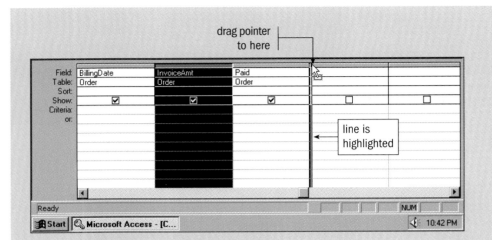

Figure 3-13
Dragging the
field in the
design grid

5. Release the mouse button. Access places the InvoiceAmt field to the right of the Paid field.

The fields are now in the correct order for the sort. Now you need to specify a descending sort order for each of the two fields.

6. Click the **Paid Sort** text box, click the **Sort** list arrow, and then click **Descending**. You've selected a descending sort order for the Paid field, which will be the primary sort key. The Paid field is a yes/no field, and a descending sort order for this type of field displays all the no (unpaid) values before the yes (paid) values.

7. Click the **InvoiceAmt Sort** text box, click the **Sort** list arrow, click **Descending**, and then click in the Criteria text box for the InvoiceAmt field. You've selected a descending sort order for the InvoiceAmt field, which will be the secondary sort key. See Figure 3-14.

Figure 3-14
Selecting two
sort keys in
Design view

primary sort key

secondary sort key

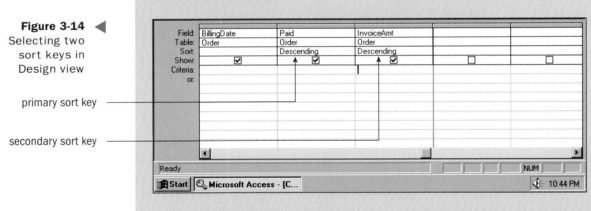

You have finished your query changes, so now you can run the query and then save the modified query with the same query name.

8. Click the **Run** button 🔳 on the Query Design toolbar. Access runs the query and displays the query datasheet. The records appear in descending order, based on the values of the Paid field. Within groups of records with the same Paid field value, the records appear in descending order by the values of the InvoiceAmt field. See Figure 3-15.

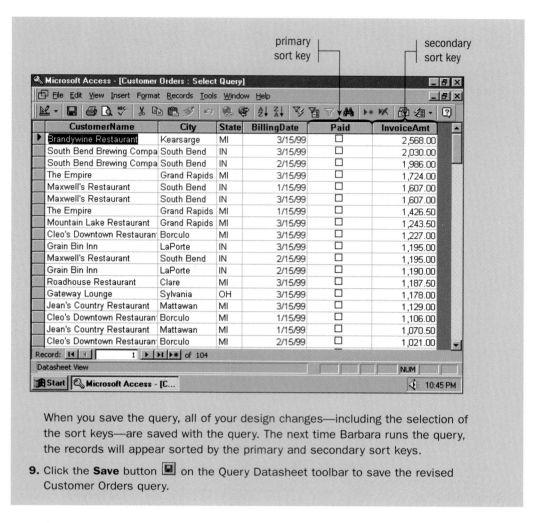

Figure 3-15 ◀
Datasheet
sorted on
two fields

When you save the query, all of your design changes—including the selection of the sort keys—are saved with the query. The next time Barbara runs the query, the records will appear sorted by the primary and secondary sort keys.

9. Click the **Save** button 🖫 on the Query Datasheet toolbar to save the revised Customer Orders query.

Barbara wants to focus her attention for a few minutes on the orders in the datasheet that are unpaid. Because selecting only the unpaid orders is a temporary change Barbara wants in the datasheet, you do not need to switch to Design view and change the query. Instead, you can apply a filter.

Filtering Data

A **filter** is a set of restrictions you place on the records in an open datasheet or form to *temporarily* isolate a subset of the records. A filter lets you view different subsets of displayed records so you can focus on only the data you need. Unless you save a query or form with a filter applied, an applied filter is not available the next time you run the query or open the form. The simplest technique for filtering records is Filter By Selection. **Filter By Selection** lets you select all or part of a field value in a datasheet or form, and then display only those records that contain the selected value in the field.

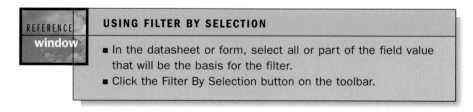

REFERENCE window	**USING FILTER BY SELECTION**
	▪ In the datasheet or form, select all or part of the field value that will be the basis for the filter.
	▪ Click the Filter By Selection button on the toolbar.

For Barbara's request, you need to select an unchecked box in the Paid field, which represents an unpaid order, and then use Filter By Selection to display only those query records with this value.

To display the records using Filter By Selection:

1. Click any check box that is unchecked in the Paid column. When you click the check box, you select the field value, but you also change the check box from unchecked to checked. Because you've changed an unpaid order to a paid order, you need to click the same check box a second time.

2. Click the same check box a second time. The field value changes back to unchecked, which is now the selected field value.

3. Click the **Filter By Selection** button 🖫 on the Query Datasheet toolbar. Access displays the filtered results. Only the 25 query records that have an unchecked Paid field value appear in the datasheet; these records are the unpaid order records. Note that the status bar display and the selected Remove Filter button on the toolbar both indicate that records have been filtered. See Figure 3-16.

Figure 3-16 ◀
Using Filter
By Selection

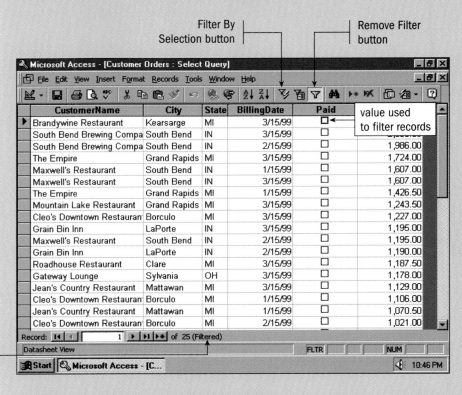

Filter By
Selection button

Remove Filter
button

indicates records
have been filtered

Barbara asks you to print the current datasheet so that she can give the printout to a staff member who is tracking unpaid orders.

4. Click the **Print** button 🖨 on the Query Datasheet toolbar. Access prints the datasheet.

   Now you can redisplay all the query records by clicking the Remove Filter button; this button works as a toggle to switch between the filtered and nonfiltered displays.

5. Click the **Remove Filter** button 🖫 on the Query Datasheet toolbar. Access redisplays all the records in the query datasheet.

6. Click the **Save** button 🖫 on the Query Datasheet toolbar, and then click the **Close** button ☒ on the menu bar to save and close the query and return to the Database window.

7. Click the **Restore** button 🗗 on the menu bar to return the Database window to its original size.

Quick Check

1 What is a select query?

2 Describe the field list and the design grid in the Query window in Design view.

3 How are a table datasheet and a query datasheet similar? How are they different?

4 The _____ is the "one" table in a one-to-many relationship, and the _____ is the "many" table in the relationship.

5 _____ is a set of rules that Access enforces to maintain consistency between related tables when you update data in a database.

6 For a date/time field, what is ascending sort order?

7 When must you define multiple sort keys in Design view instead of in the query datasheet?

8 A(n) _____ is a set of restrictions you place on the records in an open datasheet or form to temporarily isolate a subset of records.

The queries you've created will help Valle Coffee employees retrieve just the information they want to view. In the next session, you'll continue to create queries to meet their information needs.

SESSION

3.2

In this session you will specify an exact match condition in a query, change a datasheet's appearance, use a comparison operator to match a range of values, use the And and Or logical operators to define multiple selection criteria for queries, and perform calculations in queries.

Barbara wants to display customer and order information for all orders billed on 1/15/99 so she can see which orders have been paid. For this request, you need to create a query that displays selected fields from the Order and Customer tables and selected records that satisfy a condition.

Defining Record Selection Criteria for Queries

Just as you can display selected fields from a table in a query datasheet, you can display selected records. To tell Access which records you want to select, you must specify a condition as part of the query. A **condition** is a criterion, or rule, that determines which records are selected. To define a condition for a field, you place the condition in the field's Criteria text box in the design grid.

A condition usually consists of an operator, often a comparison operator, and a value. A **comparison operator** asks Access to compare the values of a database field to the condition value and to select all the records for which the relationship is true. For example, the condition >1000.00 for the InvoiceAmt field selects all records in the Order table having InvoiceAmt field values greater than 1000.00. The Access comparison operators are shown in Figure 3-17.

Figure 3-17 ◀
Access
comparison
operators

Operator	Meaning	Example
=	equal to (optional, default operator)	="Hall"
<	less than	<#1/1/94#
<=	less than or equal to	<=100
>	greater than	>"C400"
>=	greater than or equal to	>=18.75
<>	not equal to	<>"Hall"
Between ... And...	between two values (inclusive)	Between 50 And 325
In ()	in a list of values	In ("Hall", "Seeger")
Like	matches a pattern that includes wildcards	Like "706*"

Specifying an Exact Match

For Barbara's request, you need to create a query that will display only those records in the Order table with the value 1/15/99 in the BillingDate field. This type of condition is called an **exact match** because the value in the specified field must match the condition exactly in order for the record to be included in the query results. You'll use the Simple Query Wizard to create the query, and then you'll specify the exact match condition.

To create the query using the Simple Query Wizard:

1. If you took a break after the previous session, make sure Access is running and the Queries tab is displayed in the Database window, and then click the **New** button.

2. Click **Simple Query Wizard** and then click the **OK** button. Access opens the first Simple Query Wizard dialog box, in which you select the tables and fields for the query.

3. Click the **Tables/Queries** list arrow, and then click **Table: Order**. The fields in the Order table appear in the Available Fields list box. See Figure 3-18.

Figure 3-18 ◀
First Simple
Query Wizard
dialog box

selected table ——————————▶

move needed
fields here

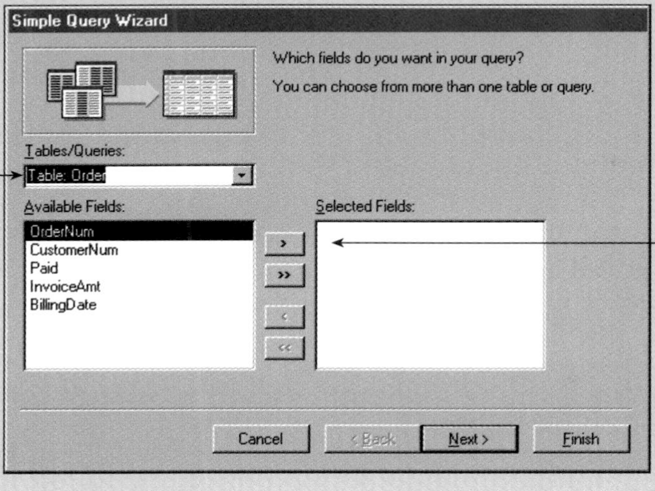

Except for the CustomerNum field, you will include all fields from the Order table in the query.

4. Click the [»] button. Access removes all the fields from the Available Fields list box and places them in the same order in the Selected Fields list box.

5. Click **CustomerNum** in the Selected Fields list box, click the [<] button to move the CustomerNum field back to the Available Fields list box, and then click **BillingDate** in the Selected Fields list box.

Barbara also wants certain information from the Customer table included in the query results.

6. Click the **Tables/Queries** list arrow, and then click **Table: Customer**. The fields in the Customer table now appear in the Available Fields list box.

7. Click **CustomerName** in the Available Fields list box, and then click the [>] button to move CustomerName to the Selected Fields list box.

8. Repeat Step 7 for the **State**, **OwnerName**, and **Phone** fields.

9. Click the **Next** button to open the second Simple Query Wizard dialog box, in which you choose whether the query will display records from the selected tables or a summary of those records. Barbara wants to view the details for the records, not a summary.

10. Make sure the **Detail** option button is selected, and then click the **Next** button to open the last Simple Query Wizard dialog box, in which you choose a name for the query and complete the wizard. You need to enter a condition for the query, so you'll want to modify the query's design.

11. Type **January Orders**, click the **Modify the query design** option button, and then click the **Finish** button. Access saves the query as January Orders and opens the query in Design view. See Figure 3-19.

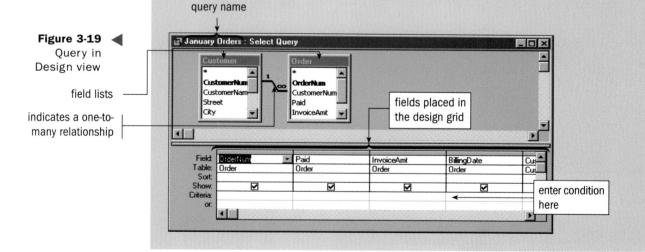

Figure 3-19 ◄
Query in
Design view

field lists

indicates a one-to-
many relationship

The field lists for the Customer and Order tables appear in the top portion of the window, and the join line indicating a one-to-many relationship connects the two tables. The selected fields appear in the design grid. Not all of the fields are visible in the grid; to see the other selected fields, you need to scroll to the right using the horizontal scroll bar.

To display the information Barbara wants, you need to enter the condition for the BillingDate field in its Criteria text box. Barbara wants to display only those records with a billing date of 1/15/99.

To enter the exact match condition, and then run the query:

1. Click the **BillingDate Criteria** text box, type **1/15/99**, and then press the **Enter** key. Access changes the condition to #1/15/99#.

   Access automatically placed number signs (#) before and after the condition. You must place date and time values inside number signs when using these values as selection criteria. If you omit the number signs, however, Access will include them automatically.

2. Click the **Run** button ![] on the Query Design toolbar. Access runs the query and displays the selected field values for only those records with a BillingDate field value of 1/15/99. A total of 36 records are selected and displayed in the datasheet. See Figure 3-20.

only records with a
BillingDate value
of 1/15/99
are selected

Figure 3-20 ◀
Datasheet
displaying
selected fields
and records

click here to
select all records

36 records selected

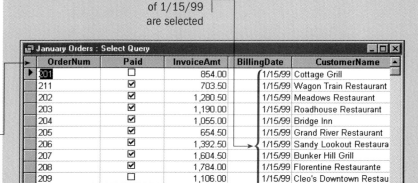

OrderNum	Paid	InvoiceAmt	BillingDate	CustomerName
201	☐	854.00	1/15/99	Cottage Grill
211	☑	703.50	1/15/99	Wagon Train Restaurant
202	☑	1,280.50	1/15/99	Meadows Restaurant
203	☑	1,190.00	1/15/99	Roadhouse Restaurant
204	☑	1,055.00	1/15/99	Bridge Inn
205	☑	654.50	1/15/99	Grand River Restaurant
206	☑	1,392.50	1/15/99	Sandy Lookout Restaura
207	☑	1,604.50	1/15/99	Bunker Hill Grill
208	☑	1,784.00	1/15/99	Florentine Restaurante
209	☐	1,106.00	1/15/99	Cleo's Downtown Restau
210	☑	1,223.00	1/15/99	Bentham's Riverfront Res
212	☑	1,220.50	1/15/99	Mountain Lake Restaurar
213	☑	1,426.50	1/15/99	Best Bet Restaurant

Record: |◀ ◀ 1 ▶ ▶| ▶* of 36

Barbara would like to see more fields and records on the screen at one time. She asks you to maximize the datasheet, change the datasheet's font size, and resize all the columns to their best fit.

Changing a Datasheet's Appearance

You can change the characteristics of a datasheet, including the font type and size of text in the datasheet, to improve its appearance or readability. You can also resize the datasheet columns to view more columns on the screen at the same time.

You'll maximize the datasheet, change the font size from the default 10 to 8, and then resize the datasheet columns.

To change the font size and resize columns in the datasheet:

1. Click the **Maximize** button ▢ on the Query window title bar.

2. Click the **record selector** to the left of the field names at the top of the datasheet (see Figure 3-20). The entire datasheet is selected.

3. Click **Format** on the menu bar, and then click **Font** to open the Font dialog box.

4. Scroll the Size list box, click **8**, and then click the **OK** button. The font size for the entire datasheet changes to 8.

   Next you need to resize the columns to their best fit—that is, so each column is just wide enough to fit the longest value in the column.

5. Position the pointer in the OrderNum field selector. When the pointer changes to ↓, click to select the entire column.

6. Click the horizontal scroll right arrow until the Phone field is fully visible, and position the pointer in the Phone field selector until the pointer changes to ↓.

7. Press and hold the **Shift** key, and then click the mouse button. All the columns are selected. Now you can resize all of them at once.

8. Position the pointer at the right edge of the Phone field selector until the pointer changes to ✛. See Figure 3-21.

Figure 3-21
Preparing to resize all columns to their best fit

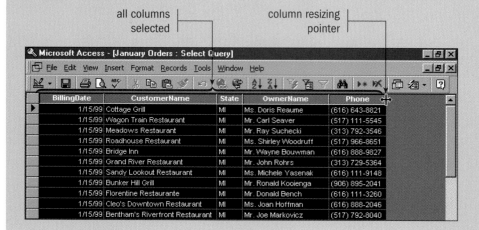

9. Double-click the mouse button. All columns are resized to their best fit, which makes each column just large enough to fit the longest *visible* field value in the column, including the field name at the top of the column. Scroll through the datasheet and resize individual columns as needed to completely display all field values.

10. If necessary, scroll to the left so that the OrderNum field is visible, and then click any field value box to deselect all columns. See Figure 3-22.

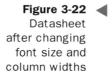

Figure 3-22
Datasheet after changing font size and column widths

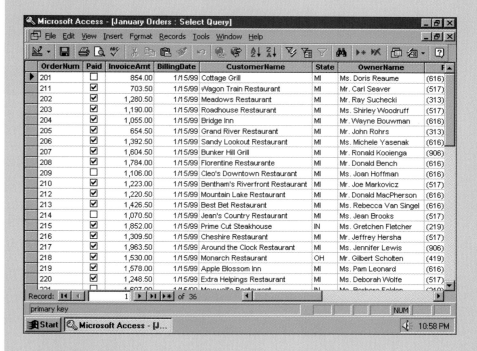

TROUBLE? Your screen might show more or fewer columns depending on the monitor you are using.

11. Click the **Save** button 🖫 on the Query Datasheet toolbar, and then click the **Close** button ☒ on the menu bar. Access saves and closes the query, and you return to the Database window.

After viewing the query results, Barbara decides that she would like to see the same fields but only for those records whose InvoiceAmt exceeds $2,000. She wants to note this information and pass it along to her staff members so that they can contact those customers with higher outstanding invoices. To create the query needed to produce these results, you need to use a comparison operator to match a range of values—in this case, any InvoiceAmt value greater than $2,000.

Using a Comparison Operator to Match a Range of Values

Once you create and save a query, you can click the Open button to run it again, or you can click the Design button to change its design. Because the design of the query you need to create next is similar to the January Orders query, you will change its design, run the query to test it, and then save the query with a new name, keeping the January Orders query intact.

To change the January Orders query design to create a new query:

1. With the January Orders query selected in the Database window, click the **Design** button. Access opens the January Orders query in Design view.

2. Click the **InvoiceAmt Criteria** text box, type **>2000**, and then press the **Tab** key. See Figure 3-23.

Figure 3-23 ◀
Changing a query's design to create a new query

new condition

condition to delete

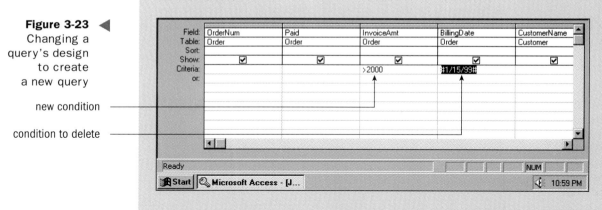

The new condition specifies that a record will be selected only if its InvoiceAmt field value exceeds 2000. Before you run the query, you need to delete the condition for the BillingDate field.

3. With the BillingDate field condition highlighted, press the **Delete** key. Access deletes the selected condition for the BillingDate field.

4. Click the **Run** button 🛈 on the Query Design toolbar. Access runs the query and displays the selected fields for only those records with an InvoiceAmt field value greater than 2000. A total of four records are selected. See Figure 3-24.

Figure 3-24 ◀
Running the modified query

only records with an InvoiceAmt value greater than 2,000 are selected

Of the records retrieved, Barbara notes that order numbers 365 and 387 have not yet been paid and the amount of each. She gives this information to her staff.

So that Barbara can display this information again, as necessary, you'll save the query as High Invoice Amounts.

5. Click **File** on the menu bar, and then click **Save As/Export** to open the Save As dialog box.

6. Type **High Invoice Amounts** in the New Name text box, and then press the **Enter** key. Access saves the query using the new query name and displays the new query name in the datasheet window title bar.

7. Click the **Close** button ⊠ on the menu bar. The Database window becomes the active window.

Leonard asks Barbara for a list of the orders billed on 1/15/99 that are still unpaid. He wants to know which customers are slow in paying their invoices. To produce this data, you need to create a query containing two conditions.

Defining Multiple Selection Criteria for Queries

Multiple conditions require you to use **logical operators** to combine two or more conditions. When you want a record selected only if two or more conditions are met, you need to use the **And logical operator**. In this case, Leonard wants to see only those records with a BillingDate field value of 1/15/99 *and* a Paid field value of No. If you place conditions in separate fields in the *same* Criteria row of the design grid, all the conditions in that row must be met in order for a record to be included in the query results. However, if you place conditions in *different* Criteria rows, Access selects a record if at least one of the conditions is met. If none of the conditions is met, then Access does not select the record. This is known as the **Or logical operator**. The difference between these two logical operators is illustrated in Figure 3-25.

Figure 3-25 ◀
Logical operators And and Or for multiple selection criteria

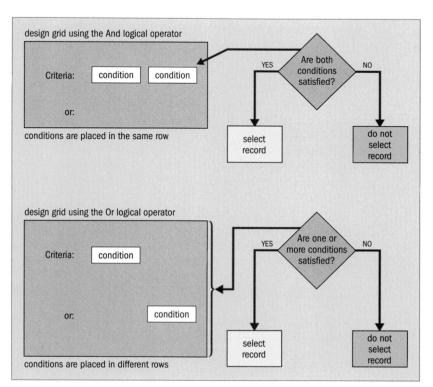

The And Logical Operator

To create the query, you need to modify the existing January Orders query to show only the unpaid orders billed on 1/15/99. For the modified query, you must add a second condition in the same Criteria row. The condition #1/15/99# for the BillingDate field finds records billed on the specified date, and the condition "No" in the Paid field finds records whose invoices have not been paid. Because the conditions appear in the same Criteria row, Access selects records only if both conditions are met.

After modifying the query, you'll save it and rename it as "Unpaid January Orders," overwriting the January Orders query, which Barbara no longer needs.

To modify the January Orders query and use the And logical operator:

1. In the Queries tab of the Database window, click **January Orders** and then click the **Design** button to open the query in Design view.

2. Click the **Paid Criteria** text box, type **no**, and then press the **Tab** key. See Figure 3-26.

Figure 3-26 ◀
Query to
find unpaid
January orders

And logical operator:
conditions entered
in the same row

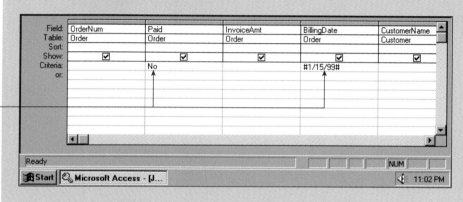

The condition for the BillingDate field is already entered, so you can run the query.

3. Click the **Run** button ⚡ on the Query Design toolbar. Access runs the query and displays in the datasheet only those records that meet both conditions: a BillingDate field value of 1/15/99 and a Paid field value of No. A total of six records are selected. See Figure 3-27.

Figure 3-27 ◀
Results of
query using the
And logical
operator

OrderNum	Paid	InvoiceAmt	BillingDate	CustomerName	State	OwnerName	Pho
201	☐	854.00	1/15/99	Cottage Grill	MI	Ms. Doris Reaume	(616) 64
209	☐	1,106.00	1/15/99	Cleo's Downtown Restaurant	MI	Ms. Joan Hoffman	(616) 88
214	☐	1,070.50	1/15/99	Jean's Country Restaurant	MI	Ms. Jean Brooks	(517) 62
221	☐	1,607.00	1/15/99	Maxwell's Restaurant	IN	Ms. Barbara Feldon	(219) 33
235	☐	1,004.50	1/15/99	Embers Restaurant	IN	Mr. Clifford Merritt	(219) 81
239	☐	1,426.50	1/15/99	The Empire	MI	Ms. Curtis Haiar	(616) 76

Now you can save the changes to the query and rename it.

4. Click the **Save** button 💾 on the Query Datasheet toolbar, and then click the **Close** button ❌ on the menu bar.

5. Right-click **January Orders** in the Queries list box, and then click **Rename** on the shortcut menu.

6. Click to position the insertion point to the left of the word "January," type **Unpaid**, press the **spacebar**, and then press the **Enter** key. The query name is now Unpaid January Orders.

Leonard also wants to determine which restaurant customers are most valuable to Valle Coffee. Specifically, he wants to see a list of those customers who have been placing orders for many years or who place orders for a substantial amount of money. He needs this information so that he can call the customers personally and thank them for their business. To create this query, you need to use the Or logical operator.

The Or Logical Operator

For Leonard's request, you need a query that selects records when either one of two conditions is satisfied or when both conditions are satisfied. That is, a record is selected if the FirstContact field value is less than 1/1/92 (to find those customers who have been doing business with Valle Coffee the longest) *or* if the InvoiceAmt field value is greater than 2000 (to find those customers who spend more money). You will enter the condition for the FirstContact field in one Criteria row and the condition for the InvoiceAmt field in another Criteria row.

To display the information Leonard wants to view, you'll create a new query containing the CustomerName, OwnerName, Phone, and FirstContact fields from the Customer table and the InvoiceAmt field from the Order table. Then you'll specify the conditions using the Or logical operator.

To create the query and use the Or logical operator:

1. From the Queries tab of the Database window, click the **New** button to open the New Query dialog box, click **Design View**, and then click the **OK** button. Access opens the Show Table dialog box on top of the Query window in Design view.

2. Click **Customer** in the Tables list box (if necessary), click the **Add** button, click **Order**, click the **Add** button, and then click the **Close** button. Access places the Customer and Order field lists in the Query window and closes the Show Table dialog box.

3. Double-click **CustomerName** in the Customer field list. Access places CustomerName in the design grid's first column Field text box.

4. Repeat Step 3 to add the **OwnerName**, **Phone**, and **FirstContact** fields from the Customer table, and then add the **InvoiceAmt** field from the Order table.

   Now you need to specify the first condition, <1/1/92, in the FirstContact field.

5. Click the **FirstContact Criteria** text box, type **<1/1/92** and then press the **Tab** key.

   Because you want records selected if either of the conditions for the FirstContact or InvoiceAmt fields is satisfied, you must enter the condition for the InvoiceAmt field in the "or" row of the design grid.

6. Press the ↓ key, and then type **>2000**. See Figure 3-28.

Figure 3-28 ◀
Query window
with the Or
logical operator

Or logical operator:
conditions entered
in different rows

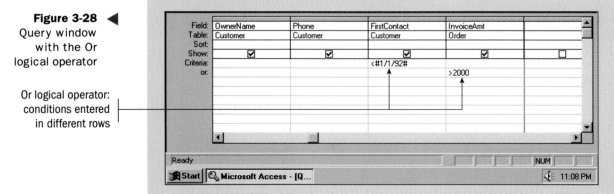

The query specifications are complete, so you can now run the query.

7. Click the **Run** button 🔳 on the Query Design toolbar. Access runs the query and displays only those records that meet either condition: a FirstContact field value less than 1/1/92 or an InvoiceAmt field value greater than 2000. A total of 35 records are selected.

Leonard wants the list displayed in alphabetical order by CustomerName.

8. Click any visible CustomerName field value to establish this field as the current field, and then click the **Sort Ascending** button 🔳 on the Query Datasheet toolbar.

9. Resize all datasheet columns to their best fit. Be sure to scroll through the entire datasheet to make sure that all values are completely displayed. See Figure 3-29.

records with
InvoiceAmt values
greater than 2,000

Figure 3-29
Results of
query using the
Or logical
operator

records with
FirstContact values
earlier than 1/1/92

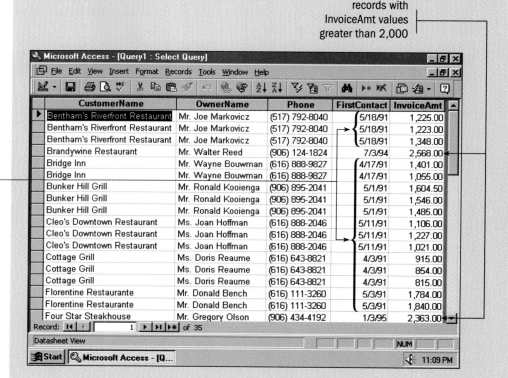

Now you'll save the query as Top Customers, print the query results, and then close the query.

10. Click the **Save** button 🔳 on the Query Datasheet toolbar, type **Top Customers** in the Query Name text box, and then press the **Enter** key. Access saves the query with the specified name in the Restaurant database.

11. Click the **Print** button 🔳 on the Query Datasheet toolbar to print the query results, and then click the **Close** button ✕ on the menu bar to close the query and return to the Database window.

Next, Leonard asks Barbara if the Restaurant database can be used to perform calculations. He is considering adding a 2% late charge to the unpaid invoices billed in January, and he wants to know exactly what these charges would be.

Performing Calculations

In addition to using queries to retrieve, sort, and filter data in a database, you can use a query to perform calculations. To perform a calculation, you define an **expression** containing a combination of database fields, constants, and operators. For numeric expressions, the data types of the database fields must be number, currency, or date/time; the constants are numbers such as .02 (for the 2% late charge); and the operators can be arithmetic operators (+ − * /) or other specialized operators. In complex expressions you can use parentheses ( ) to indicate which calculation should be performed first. In expressions without parentheses, Access calculates in the following order of precedence: multiplication and division before addition and subtraction. Access calculates operators that have equal precedence in order from left to right.

To perform a calculation in a query, you add a calculated field to the query. A **calculated field** is a field that displays the results of an expression. A calculated field appears in a query datasheet but does not exist in a database. When you run a query that contains a calculated field, Access evaluates the expression defined by the calculated field and displays the resulting value in the datasheet.

Creating a Calculated Field

To produce the information Leonard wants, you need to open the Unpaid January Orders query and create a calculated field that will multiply each InvoiceAmt field value by .02 to account for the 2% late charge Leonard is considering.

To enter an expression for a calculated field, you can type it directly in a Field text box in the design grid. Alternatively, you can open the Zoom box or Expression Builder and use either one to enter the expression. The **Zoom box** is a large text box for entering text, expressions, or other values. **Expression Builder** is an Access tool that contains an expression box for entering the expression, buttons for common operators, and one or more lists of expression elements, such as table and field names. Unlike a Field text box, which is too small to show an entire expression at one time, the Zoom box and Expression Builder are large enough to display lengthy expressions. In most cases Expression Builder provides the easiest way to enter expressions.

REFERENCE window	**USING EXPRESSION BUILDER**
	■ Display the query in Design view.
	■ In the design grid, position the insertion point in the Field text box of the field for which you want to create an expression.
	■ Click the Build button on the Query Design toolbar.
	■ Use the expression elements and common operators to build the expression.
	■ Click the OK button.

You'll begin by opening the Unpaid January Orders query in Design view and modifying it to show only the information Leonard wants to view.

To modify the Unpaid January Orders query:

   1. In the Queries tab, click **Unpaid January Orders**, and then click the **Design** button.

   Leonard wants to see only the OrderNum, CustomerName, and InvoiceAmt fields. So, you'll first delete the unnecessary fields, and then uncheck the Show boxes for the Paid and BillingDate fields. You need to keep these two fields in the query because they specify the conditions for the query; however, they do not have to be included in the query results.

2. Scroll the design grid to the right until the last three fields—State, OwnerName, and Phone—are visible.

3. Position the pointer on the State field until the pointer changes to ↓, click and hold down the mouse button, drag the mouse to the right to highlight the State, OwnerName, and Phone fields, and then release the mouse button.

4. Press the **Delete** key to delete the three selected fields.

5. Scroll the design grid back to the left, click the **Show** check box for the Paid field to remove the check mark, and then click the **Show** check box for the BillingDate field to remove the check mark.

Next, you'll move the InvoiceAmt field to the right of the CustomerName field so that the InvoiceAmt values will appear next to the calculated field values in the query results.

6. Make sure both the InvoiceAmt field and the empty field to the right of the CustomerName field are visible in the design grid.

7. Select the InvoiceAmt field, and then use the pointer ⤧ to drag the field to the right of the CustomerName field.

8. If necessary, scroll the design grid so that the empty field to the right of InvoiceAmt is visible, and then click anywhere in the design grid to deselect the InvoiceAmt field. See Figure 3-30.

Figure 3-30 ◄
Modified query
before adding
the calculated
field

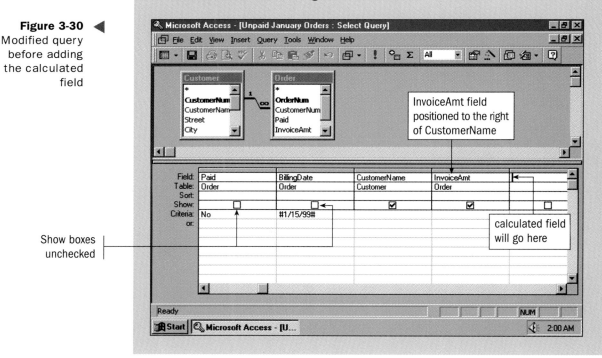

Now you're ready to use Expression Builder to enter the calculated field in the Unpaid January Orders query.

To add the calculated field to the Unpaid January Orders query:

1. Position the insertion point in the Field text box to the right of the InvoiceAmt field, and then click the **Build** button ▣ on the Query Design toolbar. The Expression Builder dialog box opens. See Figure 3-31.

Figure 3-31 ◀
Initial
Expression
Builder dialog
box

expression box

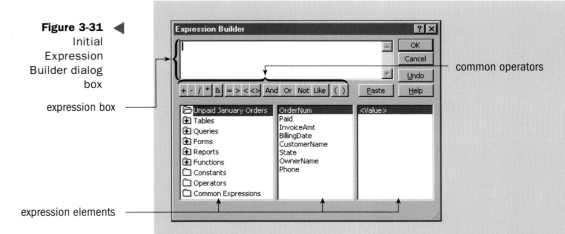

common operators

expression elements

You use the common operators and expression elements to help you build an expression. Note that the Unpaid January Orders query is already selected in the list box on the bottom left; the fields included in the query are listed in the center box.

The expression for the calculated field will multiply the InvoiceAmt field values by the numeric constant .02 (which represents a 2% late charge). To include a field in the expression, you select the field and then click the Paste button. To include a numeric constant, you simply type the constant in the expression.

2. Click **InvoiceAmt** and then click the **Paste** button. Access places [InvoiceAmt] in the expression box.

To include the multiplication operator in the expression, you click the asterisk (*) button.

3. Click the * button in the row of common operators, and then type **.02**. You have completed the entry of the expression. See Figure 3-32.

Figure 3-32 ◀
Completed
expression for
the calculated
field

expression

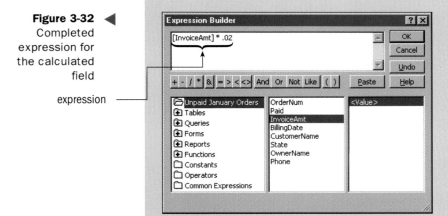

4. Click the **OK** button. Access closes the Expression Builder dialog box and adds the expression to the design grid.

Next, you need to specify a name for the calculated field as it will appear in the query results.

5. Press the **Home** key to position the insertion point to the left of the expression.

You'll enter the name LateCharge, which is descriptive of the field's contents; then you'll run the query.

6. Type **LateCharge**. Make sure you keep the colon following the field name. The colon is used to separate the field name from its expression.

   Now you can run the query.

7. Click the **Run** button ⏺ on the Query Design toolbar. Access runs the query and displays the query datasheet, which contains the three specified fields and the calculated field. See Figure 3-33.

Figure 3-33 ◀
Datasheet
displaying the
calculated field

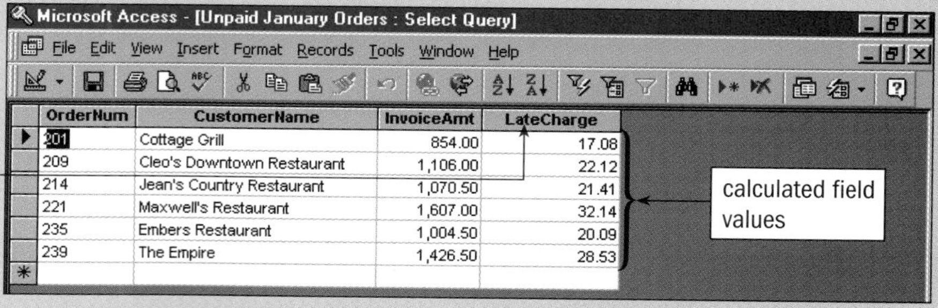

specified name for
calculated field

You'll save the query as Unpaid With Late Charge, and then close the query.

8. Click **File** on the menu bar, click **Save As/Export**, type **Unpaid With Late Charge**, press the **Enter** key, and then click the **Close** button ☒ on the menu bar. The Database window becomes the active window.

Barbara prepares a report of Valle Coffee's restaurant business for Leonard on a regular basis. The information in the report includes a summary of the restaurant orders. Barbara lists the total invoice amount for all orders, the average invoice amount, and the total number of orders. She asks you to create a query to determine these statistics from data in the Order table.

Using Aggregate Functions

You can calculate statistical information, such as totals and averages, on the records selected in a query. To do this, you use the Access aggregate functions. **Aggregate functions** perform arithmetic operations on selected records in a database. Figure 3-34 lists the most frequently used aggregate functions. Aggregate functions operate on the records that meet a query's selection criteria. You specify an aggregate function for a specific field, and the appropriate operation applies to that field's values for the selected records.

Figure 3-34 ◀
Frequently used
aggregate
functions

Aggregate Function	Determines	Data Types Supported
Avg	Average of the field values for the selected records	AutoNumber, Currency, Date/Time, Number
Count	Number of records selected	AutoNumber, Currency, Date/Time, Memo, Number, OLE Object, Text, Yes/No
Max	Highest field value for the selected records	AutoNumber, Currency, Date/Time, Number, Text
Min	Lowest field value for the selected records	AutoNumber, Currency, Date/Time, Number, Text
Sum	Total of the field values for the selected records	AutoNumber, Currency, Date/Time, Number

To display the total, average, and count of all the invoice amounts in the Order table, you will use the Sum, Avg, and Count aggregate functions for the InvoiceAmt field.

To calculate the total, average, and count of all invoice amounts:

1. Click the **New** button to open the New Query dialog box, click **Design View** (if necessary), and then click the **OK** button. Access opens the Show Table dialog box on top of the Query window in Design view.

2. Click **Order**, click the **Add** button, and then click the **Close** button. Access adds the Order field list to the top of the Query window and closes the dialog box.

   To perform the three calculations on the InvoiceAmt field, you need to add the field three times to the design grid.

3. Double-click **InvoiceAmt** in the Order field list three times to add three copies of the field to the design grid.

   You need to select an aggregate function for each InvoiceAmt field. When you click the Totals button on the Query Design toolbar, Access adds a row labeled "Total" to the design grid. The Total row provides a list of the aggregate functions that can be selected.

4. Click the **Totals** button 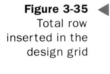 on the Query Design toolbar. Access inserts a row labeled "Total" between the Table and Sort rows in the design grid. See Figure 3-35.

Figure 3-35 ◄
Total row
inserted in the
design grid

Total row ──────→

Totals
button

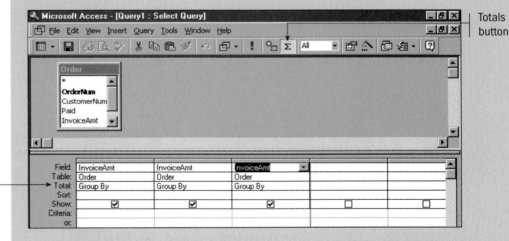

In the Total row, you specify the aggregate function you want to use for a field.

5. Click the right side of the first column's **Total** text box, and then click **Sum**. This field will calculate the total of all the InvoiceAmt field values.

   Access automatically assigns a datasheet column name of "SumOfInvoice Amount" for this field. You can change the datasheet column name to a more descriptive or readable name by entering the name you want in the Field text box. However, you must also keep InvoiceAmt in the Field text box because it identifies the field whose values will be summed. The Field text box will contain the datasheet column name you specify followed by the field name (InvoiceAmt) with a colon separating the two names.

6. Position the insertion point to the left of InvoiceAmt in the first column's Field text box, and then type **Total of Invoices:**. Be sure you include the colon at the end.

7. Click the right side of the second column's **Total** text box, and then click **Avg**. This field will calculate the average of all the InvoiceAmt field values.

8. Position the insertion point to the left of InvoiceAmt in the second column's Field text box, and then type **Average of Invoices:**.

9. Click the right side of the third column's **Total** text box, and then click **Count**. This field will calculate the total number of invoices (orders).

10. Position the insertion point to the left of InvoiceAmt in the third column's Field text box, and then type **Number of Invoices:**.

The query design is complete, so you can run the query.

11. Click the **Run** button � on the Query Design toolbar. Access runs the query and displays one record containing the three aggregate function values. The one row of summary statistics represents calculations based on the 104 records selected in the query.

You need to resize the three columns to their best fit to see the column names.

12. Resize each column by double-clicking the ✛ on the right edge of each column's field selector; then position the insertion point at the start of the field value in the first column. See Figure 3-36.

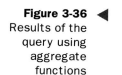
Figure 3-36
Results of the query using aggregate functions

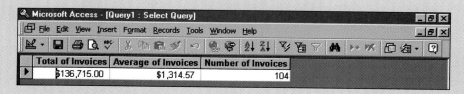

Total of Invoices	Average of Invoices	Number of Invoices
$136,715.00	$1,314.57	104

You'll save the query as Invoice Statistics.

13. Click the **Save** button 🖫 on the Query Datasheet toolbar, type **Invoice Statistics**, and then press the **Enter** key.

Barbara's report to Leonard also includes the same invoice statistics (total, average, and count) for each month. Because Valle Coffee sends invoices to their restaurant customers once a month, each invoice in a month has the same billing date. Barbara asks you to display the invoice statistics for each different billing date in the Order table.

Using Record Group Calculations

In addition to calculating statistical information on all or selected records in selected tables, you can calculate statistics for groups of records. For example, you can determine the number of customers in each state or the total invoice amounts by billing date.

To create a query for Barbara's latest request, you can modify the current query by adding the BillingDate field and assigning the Group By operator to it. The **Group By operator** divides the selected records into groups based on the values in the specified field. Those records with the same value for the field are grouped together, and the datasheet displays one record for each group. Aggregate functions, which appear in the other columns of the design grid, provide statistical information for each group.

You need to modify the current query to add the Group By operator for the BillingDate field. This will display the statistical information grouped by billing date for the 104 selected records in the query.

To add the BillingDate field with the Group By operator, and then run the query:

1. Click the **View** button for Design view 🖾 on the Query Datasheet toolbar to switch to Design view.

2. Scroll the Order field list, if necessary, and then double-click **BillingDate** to add the field to the design grid. Group By, which is the default option in the Total row, appears for the BillingDate field.

You've completed the query changes, so you can run the query.

3. Click the **Run** button ⚡ on the Query Design toolbar. Access runs the query and displays three records, one for each BillingDate group. Each record contains the three aggregate function values and the BillingDate field value for the group. Again, the summary statistics represent calculations based on the 104 records selected in the query. See Figure 3-37.

Figure 3-37 ◀
Aggregate functions grouped by BillingDate

aggregate function results

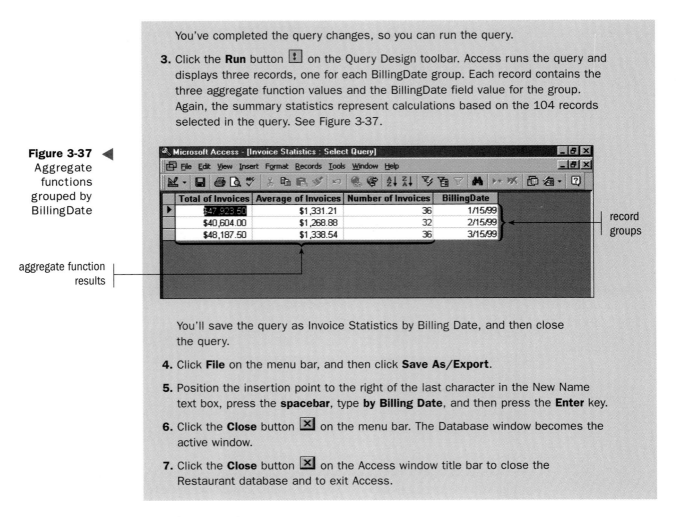

Total of Invoices	Average of Invoices	Number of Invoices	BillingDate
$47,923.50	$1,331.21	36	1/15/99
$40,604.00	$1,268.88	32	2/15/99
$48,187.50	$1,338.54	36	3/15/99

record groups

You'll save the query as Invoice Statistics by Billing Date, and then close the query.

4. Click **File** on the menu bar, and then click **Save As/Export**.

5. Position the insertion point to the right of the last character in the New Name text box, press the **spacebar**, type **by Billing Date**, and then press the **Enter** key.

6. Click the **Close** button ☒ on the menu bar. The Database window becomes the active window.

7. Click the **Close** button ☒ on the Access window title bar to close the Restaurant database and to exit Access.

Quick Check

[1] A(n) _____ is a criterion, or rule, that determines which records are selected for a query datasheet.

[2] In the design grid, where do you place the conditions for two different fields when you use the And logical operator? The Or logical operator?

[3] To perform a calculation in a query, you define a(n) _____ containing a combination of database fields, constants, and operators.

[4] How does a calculated field differ from a table field?

[5] What is an aggregate function?

[6] The _____ operator divides selected records into groups based on the values in a field.

The queries you've created and saved will help Leonard, Barbara, Kim, and other employees monitor and analyze the business activity of Valle Coffee's restaurant customers. The queries can be run at any time, modified as needed, or used as the basis for designing new queries to meet additional information requirements.

Tutorial Assignments

Barbara needs information from the Valle Products database, and she asks you to query the database by completing the following:

1. Make sure your Student Disk is in the disk drive, start Access, and then open the Valle Products database located in the TAssign folder on your Student Disk.

2. Create a select query based on the Product table. Display the ProductCode, WeightCode, and Price fields in the query results; sort in descending order based on the Price field values; and select only those records whose CoffeeCode value equals COLA. (*Hint:* Do not display the CoffeeCode field values in the query results.) Save the query as COLA Coffee, run the query, print the query datasheet, and then close the query.

3. Define a one-to-many relationship between the primary Coffee table and the related Product table, and then define a one-to-many relationship between the primary Weight table and the related Product table. (*Hint:* Add all three tables to the Relationships window, and then define the two relationships.) Select the referential integrity option and both cascade options for both relationships.

4. Create a select query based on the Coffee, Product, and Weight tables. Display the CoffeeType, CoffeeName, ProductCode, Price, and Weight/Size fields in that order. Sort in ascending order based on the CoffeeName field values. Select only those records whose CoffeeType equals "Special Import." Save the query as Special Imports, and then run the query. Resize all columns in the datasheet to fit the data. Print the datasheet and then close the query.

5. Create a query based on the Product table that shows all products that do not have a WeightCode field value of B, and whose Price field value is less than 30; display all fields except Decaf from the Product table. Save the query as Pricing, and then run the query.

6. Open the Pricing query in Design view. Create a calculated field named NewPrice that displays the results of increasing the Price values by 4%. Display the results in descending order by NewPrice. Save the query as New Prices, run the query, print the query datasheet, and then close the query.

7. Open the Special Imports query in Design view. Modify the query to display only those records with a CoffeeType field value of Special Import or with a Price field value greater than 50. Run the query, and then resize all columns in the datasheet to fit the data. Save the query as Special Imports Plus Higher Priced, print the query datasheet, and then close the query.

8. Create a new query based on the Product table. Use the Min and Max aggregate functions to find the lowest and highest values in the Price field. Name the two aggregate fields Lowest Price and Highest Price, respectively. Save the query as Lowest And Highest Prices, run the query, and then print the query datasheet.

9. Open the Lowest And Highest Prices query in Design view. Use the Show Table button on the Query Design toolbar to display the Show Table dialog box; then add the Weight table to the query. Modify the query so that the records are grouped by the Weight/Size field. Save the query as Lowest And Highest Prices By Weight/Size, run the query, print the query datasheet, and then close the query. Close the Valle Products database.

Case Problems

1. Ashbrook Mall Information Desk Sam Bullard wants to view specific information about jobs available at the Ashbrook Mall. He asks you to query the MallJobs database by completing the following:

1. Make sure your Student Disk is in the disk drive, start Access, and then open the MallJobs database located in the Cases folder on your Student Disk.

2. Define a one-to-many relationship between the primary Store table and the related Job table. Select the referential integrity option and both cascade options for the relationship.

3. Create a select query based on the Store and Job tables. Display the StoreName, Location, Position, and Hours/Week fields, in that order. Sort in ascending order based on the StoreName field values. Run the query, save the query as Store Jobs, and then print the datasheet.

4. Use Filter By Selection to temporarily display only those records with a Location field value of D1 in the Store Jobs query datasheet. Print the datasheet and then remove the filter.

5. Open the Store Jobs query in Design view. Modify the query to display only those records with a Position value of Clerk. Run the query, save the query as Clerk Jobs, and then print the datasheet.

6. Open the Clerk Jobs query in Design view. Modify the query to display only those records with a Position value of Clerk and with an Hours/Week value of 20-30. Run the query, save it with the same name, print the datasheet, and then close the query. Close the MallJobs database.

2. Professional Litigation User Services Raj Jawahir is completing an analysis of the payment history of PLUS clients. To help him find the information he needs, you'll query the Payments database by completing the following:

1. Make sure your Student Disk is in the disk drive, start Access, and then open the Payments database located in the Cases folder on your Student Disk.

2. Define a one-to-many relationship between the primary Firm table and the related Payment table. Select the referential integrity option and both cascade options for the relationship.

3. Create a select query based on the Firm and Payment tables. Display the Firm#, FirmName, AmtPaid, and DatePaid fields, in that order. Sort in descending order based on the AmtPaid field values. Select only those records whose AmtPaid is greater than 2,400.00. Save the query as Large Payments, and then run the query. Print the datasheet and then close the query.

4. For all payments on 6/2/99, display the Payment#, AmtPaid, DatePaid, and FirmName fields. Save the query as June 2 Payments, and then run the query. Switch to Design view, modify the query so that the DatePaid values do not appear in the query results, and then save the modified query. Run the query, print the query results, and then close the query.

5. For all firms that have Nancy Martinez as a PLUS account representative, display the FirmName, FirmContact, AmtPaid, and DatePaid fields. Save the query as Martinez Accounts, run the query, print the query results, and then close the query.

6. For all payments made on 6/11/99 or 6/12/99, display the DatePaid, AmtPaid, FirmName, and Firm# fields. Display the results in ascending order by DatePaid and then in descending order by AmtPaid. Save the query as Selected Dates, run the query, print the query datasheet, and then close the query.

7. Use the Payment table to display the highest, lowest, total, average, and count of the AmtPaid field for all payments. Then do the following:
   a. Specify column names of HighestPayment, LowestPayment, TotalPayments, AveragePayment, and #Payments. Save the query as Payment Statistics, and then run the query. Resize all datasheet columns to their best fit, and then print the query results.
   b. Change the query to display the same statistics by DatePaid. Save the query as Payment Statistics By Date, run the query, and then print the query results.
   c. Change the Payment Statistics By Date query to display the same statistics by DatePaid then by Deposit#. Save the query as Payment Statistics By Date By Deposit, print the query results using landscape orientation, and then close the query. Close the Payments database.

3. Best Friends Noah and Sheila Warnick want to find specific information about the Walk-A-Thons they conduct for Best Friends. You'll help them find the information in the Walks database by completing the following:

1. Make sure your Student Disk is in the disk drive, start Access, and then open the Walks database located in the Cases folder on your Student Disk.

2. Define a one-to-many relationship between the primary Walker table and the related Pledge table. Select the referential integrity option and both cascade options for the relationship.

3. For all walkers with a PledgeAmt field value of greater than 20, display the WalkerID, LastName, Pledge#, and PledgeAmt fields. Sort the query in descending order by PledgeAmt. Save the query as Large Pledges, run the query, print the query datasheet, and then close the query.

4. For all walkers who pledged less than $10 or who pledged $5 per mile, display the Pledger, PledgeAmt, PerMile, LastName, and FirstName fields. Save the query as Pledged Or Per Mile, run the query, and then print the query datasheet. Change the query to select all walkers who pledged less than $10 and who pledged $5 per mile. Save the query as Pledged And Per Mile, and then run the query. Describe the results. Close the query.

5. For all pledges, display the Pledger, Distance, PerMile, and PledgeAmt fields. Save the query as Difference. Create a calculated field named CalcPledgeAmt that displays the results of multiplying the Distance and PerMile fields; then save the query. Create a second calculated field named Difference that displays the results of subtracting the CalcPledgeAmt field from the PledgeAmt field. Format the calculated fields as fixed with two decimal places. (*Hint:* Choose the Properties option on the shortcut menu for the selected fields.) Display the results in ascending order by PledgeAmt. Save the modified query, and then run the query. Resize all datasheet columns to their best fit, print the query results, and then close the query.

6. Use the Pledge table to display the total, average, and count of the PledgeAmt field for all pledges. Then do the following:
   a. Specify column names of TotalPledge, AveragePledge, and #Pledges.

   b. Change properties so that the values in the TotalPledge and AveragePledge columns display two decimal places and the fixed format. (*Hint:* Choose the Properties option on the shortcut menu for the selected field.)
   c. Save the query as Pledge Statistics, run the query, resize all datasheet columns to their best fit, and then print the query datasheet.

   d. Change the query to display the sum, average, and count of the PledgeAmt field for all pledges by LastName. (*Hint:* Use the Show Table button on the Query Design toolbar to add the Walker table to the query.) Save the query as Pledge Statistics By Walker, run the query, print the query datasheet, and then close the query. Close the Walks database.

4. Lopez Lexus Dealerships Maria and Hector Lopez want to analyze data about the cars and different locations for their Lexus dealerships. Help them query the Lexus database by completing the following:

1. Make sure your Student Disk is in the disk drive, start Access, and then open the Lexus database located in the Cases folder on your Student Disk.

2. Define a one-to-many relationship between the primary Locations table and the related Cars table. Select the referential integrity option and both cascade options for the relationship.

3. For all vehicles, display the Model, Year, LocationCode, and SellingPrice fields. Save the query as Car Info, and then run the query. Resize all datasheet columns to their best fit. In Datasheet view, sort the query results in ascending order by the SellingPrice field. Print the query datasheet, and then save and close the query.

4. For all vehicles manufactured in 1998, display the Model, Year, Cost, SellingPrice, and LocationName fields. Sort the query in descending order by Cost. Save the query as 1998 Cars, and then run the query. Modify the query to remove the display of the Year field values from the query results. Save the modified query, run the query, print the query datasheet, and then close the query.

5. For all vehicles located in Houston or with a transmission of A4, display the Model, Year, Cost, SellingPrice, Transmission, LocationCode, and LocationName fields. Save the query as Location Or Trans, run the query, and then print the query datasheet using landscape orientation. Change the query to select all vehicles located in Houston and with a transmission of A4. Save the query as Location And Trans, run the query, print the query datasheet in landscape orientation, and then close the query.

6. For all vehicles, display the Model, Year, Cost, and SellingPrice fields. Save the query as Profit. Then create a calculated field named Profit that displays the difference between the vehicle's selling price and cost. Display the results in descending order by Profit. Save the query, run the query, print the query datasheet, and then close the query.

7. Use the Cars table to determine the total cost, average cost, total selling price, and average selling price of all vehicles. Use the Index tab in online Help to look up the word "caption"; then choose the topic "Change a field name in a query." Read the displayed information, and then choose and read the subtopic "Display new field names by changing the Caption property." Close the Help window. Set the Caption property of the four fields to Total Cost, Average Cost, Total Selling Price, and Average Selling Price, respectively. Save the query as Car Statistics, run the query, resize all datasheet columns to their best fit, and then print the query datasheet. Revise the query to show the car statistics by LocationName. (*Hint:* Use the Show Table button on the Query Design toolbar to display the Show Table dialog box.) Set the Caption property of the LocationName field to Location. Save the revised query as Car Statistics By Location, run the query, print the query datasheet, and then close the query.

8. Use the Office Assistant to ask the following question: "How do I create a Top Values query?" Choose the topic "Display only the highest or lowest values in the query's results." Read the displayed information, and then close the Help window and the Office Assistant. Open the Profit query in Design view, and then modify the query to display only the top five values for the Profit field. Save the query as Top Profit, run the query, print the query datasheet, and then close the query. Close the Lexus database.

Creating Forms and Reports

Creating an Order Data Form, a Customer Orders Form, and a Customers and Orders Report

CASE

Valle Coffee

Barbara Hennessey wants to continue to enhance the Restaurant database to make it easier for her office staff members and other Valle Coffee employees to find and maintain data. In particular, she wants the database to include a form for the Order table, similar to the Customer Data form, which is based on the Customer table. She also wants a form that shows data from both the Customer and Order tables at the same time, so that all the order information for each customer appears with the corresponding customer data, giving a complete picture of the restaurant customers and their orders.

In addition, Kim Carpenter would like a report showing customer and order data so that her marketing staff members have printed output to refer to when completing market analyses and planning strategies for selling to restaurant customers. She wants the information to be formatted attractively, perhaps including the Valle Coffee cup logo on the report for visual interest.

SESSION 4.1

In this session you will create a form using the Form Wizard, change a form's AutoFormat, navigate a form, find data using a form, print selected form records, and maintain table data using a form.

Creating a Form Using the Form Wizard

As you learned in Tutorial 1, a form is an object you use to maintain, view, and print records in a database. In Access, you can design your own forms or use Form Wizards to create them for you automatically.

Barbara asks you to create a new form her staff can use to view and maintain data in the Order table. In Tutorial 1, you used the AutoForm Wizard, which creates a form automatically using all the fields in the selected table or query, to create the Customer Data form. To create the form for the Order table, you'll use the Form Wizard. The **Form Wizard** allows you to choose some or all of the fields in the selected table or query, choose fields from other tables and queries, and display the chosen fields in any order on the form. You can also choose a style for the form.

To open the Restaurant database and activate the Form Wizard:

1. Place your Student Disk in the appropriate disk drive.
2. Start Access and open the Restaurant database located in the Tutorial folder on your Student Disk. The Restaurant database is displayed in the Access window.
3. Click the **Forms** tab in the Database window to select the tab. The Forms list includes the Customer Data form you created in Tutorial 1.
4. Click the **New** button in the Database window. The New Form dialog box opens.
5. Click **Form Wizard**, click the list arrow for choosing a table or query, click **Order** to select this table as the source for the form, and then click the **OK** button. The first Form Wizard dialog box opens. See Figure 4-1.

Figure 4-1 First Form Wizard dialog box

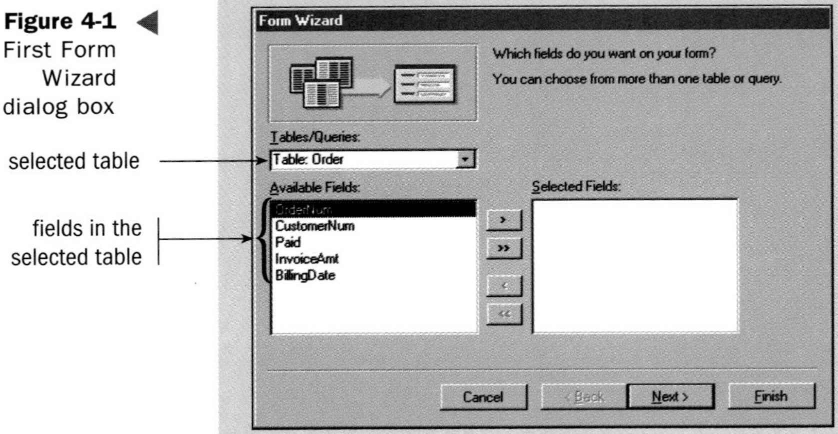

Barbara wants the form to display all the fields in the Order table, but in a different order. She would like the Paid field to be placed at the bottom of the form so that it stands out more, making it easier to determine if an order has been paid.

To finish creating the form using the Form Wizard:

1. Click **OrderNum** in the Available Fields list box (if necessary), and then click the [>] button to move the field to the Selected Fields list box.

2. Repeat Step 1 to select the **CustomerNum**, **InvoiceAmt**, **BillingDate**, and **Paid** fields, in that order.

3. Click the **Next** button to display the second Form Wizard dialog box, in which you select a layout for the form. See Figure 4-2.

Figure 4-2 ◀
Choosing a
layout for
the form

sample of the
selected layout

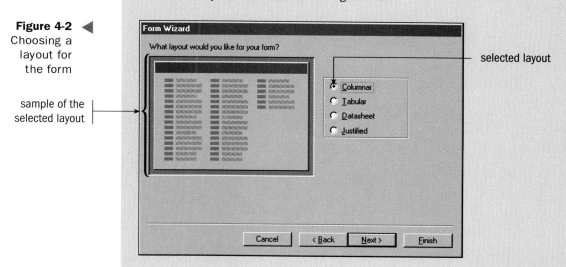

selected layout

The layout choices are columnar, tabular, datasheet, and justified. A sample of the selected layout appears on the left side of the dialog box.

4. Click each of the option buttons and review the corresponding sample layout.

The tabular and datasheet layouts display the fields from multiple records at one time, whereas the columnar and justified layouts display the fields from one record at a time. Barbara thinks the columnar layout is the appropriate arrangement for displaying and updating data in the table, so you'll choose this layout.

5. Click the **Columnar** option button (if necessary), and then click the **Next** button. Access displays the third Form Wizard dialog box, in which you choose a style for the form. See Figure 4-3.

Figure 4-3 ◀
Choosing a
style for
the form

sample of the
selected style

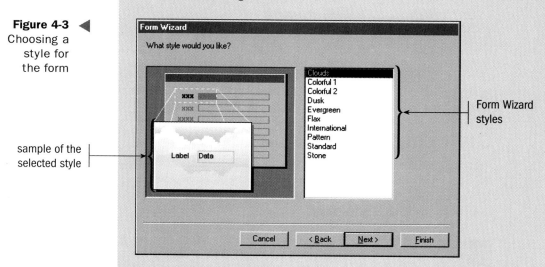

Form Wizard
styles

A sample of the selected style appears in the box on the left. If you choose a style, which is called an *AutoFormat*, and decide you'd prefer a different one after the form is created, you can change it.

6. Click each of the styles and review the corresponding sample.

Barbara likes the Evergreen style and asks you to use it for the form.

7. Click **Evergreen** and then click the **Next** button. Access displays the final Form Wizard dialog box and shows the table name as the default for the form name and for the title that will appear in the form title bar. See Figure 4-4.

Figure 4-4 ◄
Final Form
Wizard
dialog box

option to
display the form

option to change
the form's design

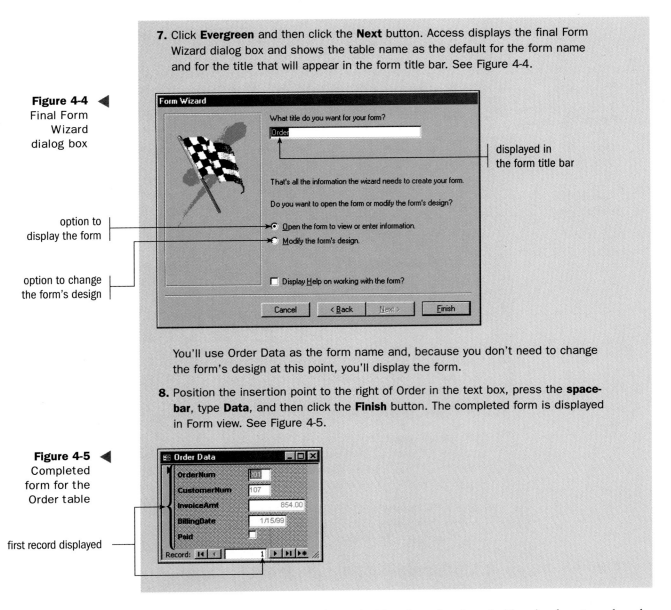

displayed in
the form title bar

You'll use Order Data as the form name and, because you don't need to change the form's design at this point, you'll display the form.

8. Position the insertion point to the right of Order in the text box, press the **space-bar**, type **Data**, and then click the **Finish** button. The completed form is displayed in Form view. See Figure 4-5.

Figure 4-5 ◄
Completed
form for the
Order table

first record displayed

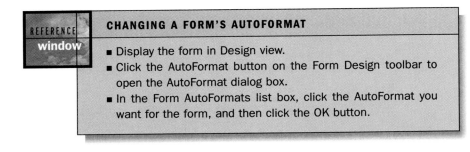

After viewing the form, Barbara decides that she doesn't like the form's style—the green background makes the field names difficult to read and the green type for the field values is too light. She asks you to change the form's style.

Changing a Form's AutoFormat

You can change a form's appearance by choosing a different AutoFormat for the form. As you learned when you created the Order Data form, an **AutoFormat** is a predefined style for a form (or report). The AutoFormats available for a form are the ones you saw when you selected the form's style using the Form Wizard. To change an AutoFormat, you must switch to Design view.

REFERENCE
window

CHANGING A FORM'S AUTOFORMAT

- Display the form in Design view.
- Click the AutoFormat button on the Form Design toolbar to open the AutoFormat dialog box.
- In the Form AutoFormats list box, click the AutoFormat you want for the form, and then click the OK button.

To change the AutoFormat for the Order Data form:

1. Click the **View** button for Design view 🖳 on the Form View toolbar. The form is displayed in Design view. See Figure 4-6.

Figure 4-6 ◀
Form displayed
in Design view

Form window

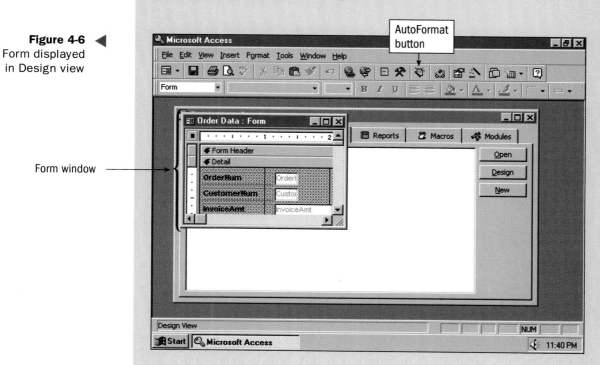

TROUBLE? If your screen displays any other windows than those shown in Figure 4-6, click the Close button ✖ on the particular window's title bar to close it.

You use Design view to modify an existing form or to create a form from scratch. In this case, you need to change the AutoFormat for the Order Data form.

2. Click the **AutoFormat** button 🗗 on the Form Design toolbar. The AutoFormat dialog box opens.

3. Click the **Options** button to display the AutoFormat options. See Figure 4-7.

Figure 4-7 ◀
AutoFormat
dialog box

AutoFormats
for forms

AutoFormat options

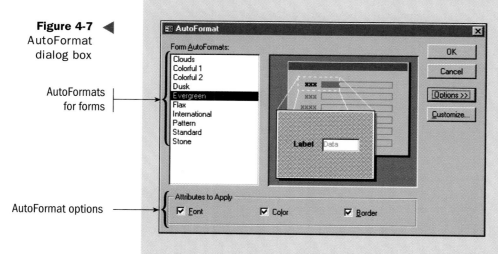

A sample of the selected AutoFormat appears to the right of the Form AutoFormats list box. The options at the bottom of the dialog box allow you to apply the selected AutoFormat or just its font, color, or border.

Barbara decides that she prefers the Standard AutoFormat, because its field names and field values are easy to read.

4. Click **Standard** in the Form AutoFormats list box, and then click the **OK** button. The AutoFormat dialog box closes, the AutoFormat is applied to the form, and the Form window in Design view becomes the active window.

5. Click the **View** button for Form view  on the Form Design toolbar. The form is displayed in Form view with the new AutoFormat. See Figure 4-8.

Figure 4-8 ◀
Form displayed
with the new
AutoFormat

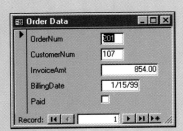

You have finished modifying the format of the form and can now save it.

6. Click the **Save** button 🖫 on the Form View toolbar to save the modified form.

Barbara wants to view some data in the Order table using the form. To view data, you need to navigate through the form.

Navigating a Form

To maintain and view data using a form, you must know how to move from field to field and from record to record. The mouse movement, selection, and placement techniques to navigate a form are the same techniques you've used to navigate a table datasheet and the Customer Data form you created in Tutorial 1. Also, the navigation mode and editing mode keystroke techniques are the same as those you used previously for datasheets (see Figure 2-29).

To navigate through the form:

1. Press the **Tab** key to move to the CustomerNum field value, and then press the **End** key to move to the Paid field. Because the Paid field is a yes/no field, its value is not highlighted; instead, a dashed box appears around the field name to indicate it is the current field.

2. Press the **Home** key to move back to the OrderNum field value. The first record in the Order table still appears in the form.

3. Press **Ctrl + End** to move to the Paid field in record 104, which is the last record in the table. The record number for the current record appears between the navigation buttons at the bottom of the form.

4. Click the **Previous Record** navigation button ◄ to move to the Paid field in record 103.

5. Press the ↑ key twice to move to the InvoiceAmt field value in record 103.

6. Position the insertion point between the numbers "2" and "6" in the InvoiceAmt field value to switch to editing mode, press the **Home** key to move the insertion point to the beginning of the field value, and then press the **End** key to move the insertion point to the end of the field value.

7. Click the **First Record** navigation button ◄◄ to move to the InvoiceAmt field value in the first record. The entire field value is highlighted because you have switched from editing mode to navigation mode.

8. Click the **Next Record** navigation button ► to move to the InvoiceAmt field value in record 2, which is the next record.

Barbara asks you to display the records for Jean's Country Restaurant, whose customer number is 407, because she wants to review the orders for this customer.

Finding Data Using a Form

The **Find** command allows you to search the data in a form and to display only those records you want to view. You choose a field to serve as the basis for the search by making that field the current field; then you enter the value you want Access to match in the Find in field dialog box. You can use the Find command for a form or datasheet, and you can activate the command from the Edit menu or by clicking the toolbar Find button.

REFERENCE window

FINDING DATA

- On a form or datasheet, click anywhere in the field value you want to search.
- Click the Find button on the toolbar to open the Find in field dialog box.
- In the Find What text box, type the field value you want to find.
- Complete the remaining options, as necessary, to specify the type of search you want Access to perform.
- Click the Find First button to have Access begin the search at the beginning of the table, or click the Find Next button to begin the search at the current record.
- Click the Find Next button to continue the search for the next match.
- Click the Close button to stop the search operation.

You need to find all records in the Order table for Jean's Country Restaurant, whose customer number is 407.

To find the records using the Order Data form:

1. Position the insertion point in the CustomerNum field value box. This is the field for which you will find matching values.

2. Click the **Find** button 🔍 on the Form View toolbar to open the Find in field dialog box. Note that the title bar of the dialog box specifies the name of the field that Access will search, in this case, the CustomerNum field.

3. If the Find in field dialog box covers any part of the form, move the dialog box by dragging its title bar. See Figure 4-9.

Figure 4-9 ◀
Find in field
dialog box

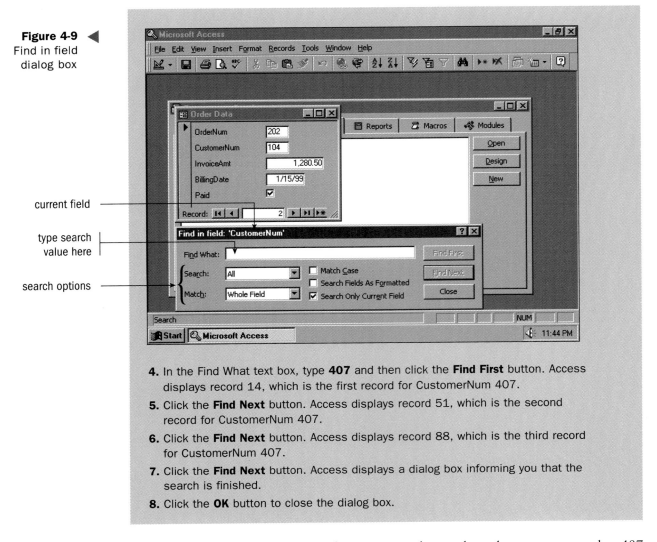

current field

type search
value here

search options

4. In the Find What text box, type **407** and then click the **Find First** button. Access displays record 14, which is the first record for CustomerNum 407.

5. Click the **Find Next** button. Access displays record 51, which is the second record for CustomerNum 407.

6. Click the **Find Next** button. Access displays record 88, which is the third record for CustomerNum 407.

7. Click the **Find Next** button. Access displays a dialog box informing you that the search is finished.

8. Click the **OK** button to close the dialog box.

The search value you enter can be an exact value, such as the customer number 407 you just entered, or it can include wildcard characters. A **wildcard character** is a placeholder you use when you know only part of a value or when you want to start or end with a specific character or match a certain pattern. Figure 4-10 shows the wildcard characters you can use when finding data.

Figure 4-10 ◀
Wildcard
characters

Wildcard Character	Purpose	Example
*	Match any number of characters. It can be used as the first and/or last character in the character string.	th* finds *the, that, this, therefore,* and so on
?	Match any single alphabetic character.	a?t finds *act, aft, ant,* and *art*
[ ]	Match any single character within the brackets.	a[fr]t finds *aft* and *art* but not *act* and *ant*
!	Match any character not within brackets.	a[!fr]t finds *act* and *ant* but not *aft* and *art*
-	Match any one of a range of characters. The range must be in ascending order (a to z, not z to a).	a[d-p]t finds aft and ant but not act and art
#	Match any single numeric character.	#72 finds *072, 172, 272, 372,* and so on

To check if their orders have been paid, Barbara wants to view the order records for two customers: Cheshire Restaurant (CustomerNum 515) and Around the Clock Restaurant (CustomerNum 597). You'll use the * wildcard character to search for these customers' orders.

To find the records using the * wildcard character:

1. Double-click **407** in the Find What text box to select the entire value, and then type **5***.

   Access will match any field value in the CustomerNum field that starts with the digit 5.

2. Click the **Find First** button. Access displays record 16, which is the first record for CustomerNum 515. Note that the Paid field value is checked, indicating that this order has been paid.

3. Click the **Find Next** button. Access displays record 17, which is the first record for CustomerNum 597.

4. Click the **Find Next** button. Access displays record 39, which is the second record for CustomerNum 597.

5. Click the **Find Next** button. Access displays record 68, which is the second record for CustomerNum 515.

6. Click the **Find Next** button. Access displays record 82, which is the third record for CustomerNum 515.

7. Click the **Find Next** button. Access displays a dialog box informing you that the search is finished.

8. Click the **OK** button to close the dialog box.

9. Click the **Close** button to close the Find in field dialog box.

All five orders have been paid, but Barbara wants to make sure Valle Coffee has a record of payment for order number 375. She asks you to print the data displayed on the form for record 82, which is for order number 375, so she can ask a staff member to look for the payment record for this order.

Previewing and Printing Selected Form Records

Access prints as many form records as can fit on a printed page. If only part of a form record fits on the bottom of a page, the remainder of the record prints on the next page. Access allows you to print all pages or a range of pages. In addition, you can print the currently selected form record.

Before printing record 82, you'll preview the form record to see how it will look when printed.

To preview the form and print the data for record 82:

1. Make sure record 82 is the current record in the Order Data form.

2. Click the **Print Preview** button 🔍 on the Form View toolbar. The Print Preview window opens, showing the form records for the Order table in miniature.

3. Click the **Maximize** button 🗖 on the form title bar.

4. Click the **Zoom** button 🔍 on the Print Preview toolbar, and then use the vertical scroll bar to view the contents of the window. See Figure 4-11.

Figure 4-11
Print Preview
window
displaying
form records

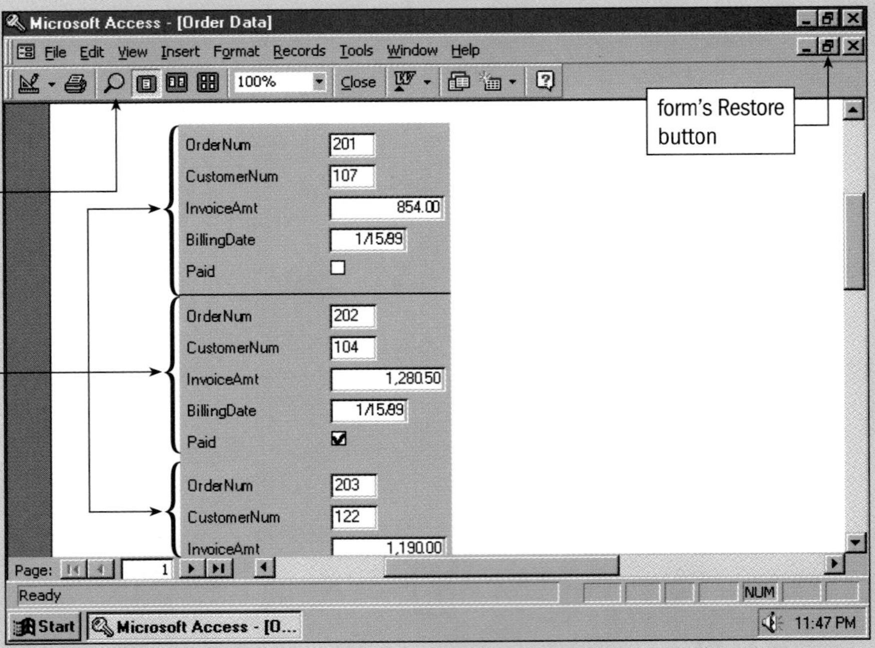

Zoom button

form records

Each record from the Order table appears in a separate form. Access places as many forms as will fit on each page.

5. Click the **Restore** button 🗗 on the Print Preview menu bar, and then click the **Close** button on the Print Preview toolbar to return to the table in Form view.

6. Click **File** on the menu bar, and then click **Print**. The Print dialog box opens.

7. Click the **Selected Record(s)** option button to print only the current form record (record 82).

8. Click the **OK** button to close the dialog box and print the selected record.

Barbara has identified several updates she wants you to make to the Order table using the Order Data form, as shown in Figure 4-12.

Figure 4-12
Updates to the
Order table

Order Number	Update Action
319	Change InvoiceAmt to 1,175.00 Change Paid to Yes
392	Delete record
400	Add new record for CustomerNum 135, InvoiceAmt of 1,350.00, BillingDate of 3/15/99, and Paid status of No

Maintaining Table Data Using a Form

Maintaining data using a form is often easier than using a datasheet, because you can concentrate on all the changes required to a single record at a time. You already know how to navigate a form and find specific records. Now you'll make the changes Barbara requested to the Order table using the Order Data form.

First, you'll update the record for OrderNum 319.

To change the record using the Order Data form:

1. Make sure the Order Data form is displayed in Form view.

   The current record number appears between the sets of navigation buttons at the bottom of the form. If you know the number of the record you want to change, you can type the number and press the Enter key to go directly to the record. When she reviewed the order data to identify possible corrections, Barbara noted that 48 is the record number for order number 319.

2. Select the number 82 that appears between the navigation buttons, type **48**, and then press the **Enter** key. Record 48 is now the current record.

   You need to change the InvoiceAmt field value to 1,175.00 and the Paid field value to Yes for this record.

3. Position the insertion point between the numbers 9 and 5 in the InvoiceAmt field value, press the **Backspace** key, and then type **7**. Note that the pencil symbol appears in the top left of the form, indicating that the form is in editing mode.

4. Press the **Tab** key twice to move to the Paid field value, and then press the **spacebar** to insert a check mark in the check box. See Figure 4-13.

Figure 4-13 ◀
Order record after changing field values

indicates editing mode

field values changed

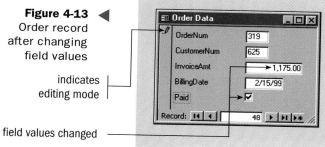

You have completed the changes for order number 319. Barbara's next update is to delete the record for order number 392. The customer who placed this order canceled it before the order was filled and processed.

To delete the record using the Order Data form:

1. Click anywhere in the OrderNum field value to make it the current field.

2. Click the **Find** button 🔍 on the Form View toolbar. The Find in field dialog box opens.

3. Type **392** in the Find What text box, click the **Find First** button, and then click the **Close** button. The record for order number 392 is now the current record.

   To delete the record, you first need to select the entire record by clicking anywhere in the large rectangular area surrounding the record selector.

4. Click the **record selector** in the top left of the form to select the entire record. See Figure 4-14.

Figure 4-14 ◀
Entire record
selected

click to select
the entire record

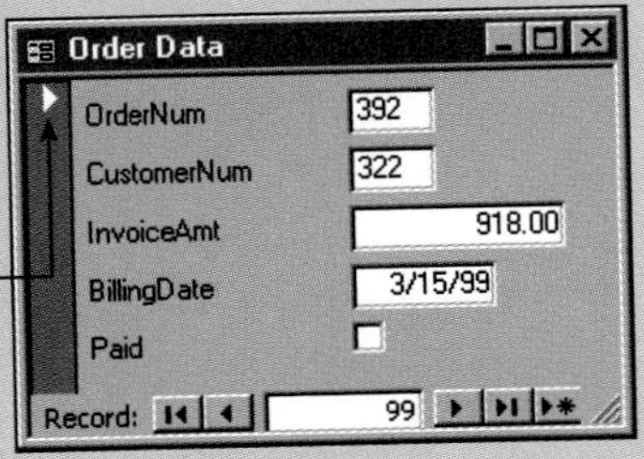

[Form screenshot: Order Data window showing OrderNum 392, CustomerNum 322, InvoiceAmt 918.00, BillingDate 3/15/99, Paid unchecked; Record: 99]

5. Click the **Delete Record** button ⬚ on the Form View toolbar. A dialog box opens, asking you to confirm the record deletion.

6. Click the **Yes** button. The dialog box closes and the record for order number 392 is deleted from the table.

Barbara's final maintenance change is to add a record for a new order placed by Topview Restaurant.

To add the new record using the Order Data form:

1. Click the **New Record** button ⬚ on the Form View toolbar. Record 104, the next record available for a new record, becomes the current record. All field value boxes are empty, and the insertion point is positioned at the beginning of the field value for OrderNum.

2. Refer to Figure 4-15 and enter the value shown for each field, pressing the Tab key to move from field to field.

Figure 4-15 ◀
Completed
form for the
new record

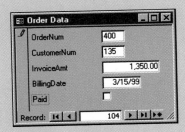

[Form screenshot: Order Data window showing OrderNum 400, CustomerNum 135, InvoiceAmt 1,350.00, BillingDate 3/15/99, Paid unchecked; Record: 104]

TROUBLE? Compare your screen with Figure 4-15. If any field value is wrong, correct it now using the methods described earlier for editing field values.

3. After entering the value for BillingDate, press the **Tab** key twice (if necessary). Record 105, the next record available for a new record, becomes the current record, and the record for order number 400 is saved in the Order table.

You've completed Barbara's changes to the Order table, so you can close the Order Data form.

4. Click the **Close** button ⬚ on the form title bar. The form closes and you return to the Database window. Notice that the Order Data form is listed in the Forms list box.

Quick Check

1 Describe the difference between creating a form using the AutoForm Wizard and creating a form using the Form Wizard.

2 What is an AutoFormat, and how do you change one for an existing form?

| 3 | Which table record is displayed in a form when you press Ctrl + End? |

3 Which table record is displayed in a form when you press Ctrl + End?

4 You can use the Find command to search for data in a form or _____.

5 Which wildcard character matches any single alphabetic character?

6 How many form records does Access print by default on a page?

7 How do you select an entire form record?

The Order Data form will enable Barbara and her staff to enter and maintain data easily in the Order table. In the next session, you'll create another form for working with data in both the Order and Customer tables at the same time. You'll also create a report showing data from both tables.

SESSION

4.2

In this session you will create a form with a main form and a subform, create a report using the Report Wizard, insert a picture on a report, preview and print a report, and compact a database.

Barbara would like you to create a form so that she can view the data for each customer and all the orders for the customer at the same time. The type of form you need to create will include a main form and a subform.

Creating a Form with a Main Form and a Subform

To create a form based on two tables, you must first define a relationship between the two tables. In Tutorial 3, you defined a one-to-many relationship between the Customer (primary) and Order (related) tables, so you are ready to create the form based on both tables.

When you create a form containing data from two tables that have a one-to-many relationship, you actually create a main form for data from the primary table and a subform for data from the related table. Access uses the defined relationship between the tables to automatically join the tables through the common field that exists in both tables.

Barbara and her staff will use the form when contacting customers about the status of their order payments. Consequently, the main form will contain the customer number and name, owner name, and phone number; the subform will contain the order number, paid status, invoice amount, and billing date.

You'll use the Form Wizard to create the form.

To activate the Form Wizard to create the form:

1. If you took a break after the previous session, make sure Access is running and the Forms tab is displayed in the Database window, and then click the **New** button. The New Form dialog box opens.

When creating a form based on two tables, you first choose the primary table and select the fields you want to include in the main form; then you choose the related table and select fields from it for the subform.

2. Click **Form Wizard**, click the list arrow for choosing a table or query, click **Customer** to select this table as the source for the main form, and then click the **OK** button. The first Form Wizard dialog box opens, in which you select fields in the order you want them to appear on the main form.

Barbara wants the form to include only the CustomerNum, CustomerName, OwnerName, and Phone fields from the Customer table.

3. Click **CustomerNum** in the Available Fields list box (if necessary), and then click the ⌐ > ⌐ button to move the field to the Selected Fields list box.

4. Repeat Step 3 for the **CustomerName**, **OwnerName**, and **Phone** fields.

The CustomerNum field will appear in the main form, so you do not have to include it in the subform. Otherwise, Barbara wants the subform to include all the fields from the Order table.

5. Click the **Tables/Queries** list arrow, and then click **Table: Order**. The fields from the Order table appear in the Available Fields list box. The quickest way to add the fields you want to include is to move all the fields to the Selected Fields list box, and then remove only the field you don't want to include (CustomerNum).

6. Click the ⌐ >> ⌐ button to move all the fields from the Order table to the Selected Fields list box.

7. Click **Order.CustomerNum** in the Selected Fields list box, and then click the ⌐ < ⌐ button to move the field back to the Available Fields list box. Note that the table name (Order) is included in the field name to distinguish it from the same field (CustomerNum) in the Customer table.

8. Click the **Next** button. The next Form Wizard dialog box opens. See Figure 4-16.

Figure 4-16 ◄
Choosing a main/subform format

primary table ————

related table ————

option for a form with a subform

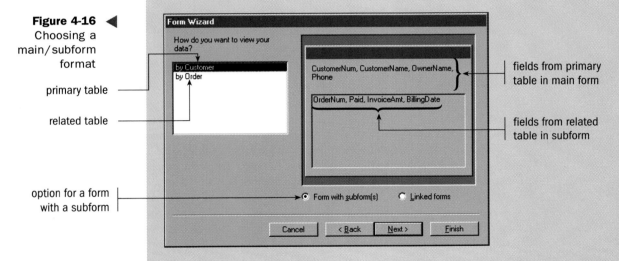

fields from primary table in main form

fields from related table in subform

In this dialog box, the list box on the left shows the order in which you will view the selected data: first by data from the Customer table (primary table), then by data from the Order table (related table). The form will be displayed as shown in the right side of the dialog box, with the fields from the Customer table at the top in the main form, and the fields from the Order table at the bottom in the subform. The selected option button specifies a main form with a subform.

The default options shown in Figure 4-16 are correct for creating a form with Customer data in the main form and Order data in the subform.

To finish creating the form:

1. Click the **Next** button. The next Form Wizard dialog box opens, in which you choose the subform layout.

The tabular layout displays subform fields as a table, whereas the datasheet layout displays subform fields as a table datasheet. The layout choice is a matter of personal preference. You'll use the datasheet layout.

2. Click the **Datasheet** option button (if necessary), and then click the **Next** button. The next Form Wizard dialog box opens, in which you choose the form's AutoFormat.

Barbara wants all forms to have the same style, so you will choose the Standard AutoFormat, which is the same AutoFormat you used to create the Order Data form earlier.

3. Click **Standard** (if necessary) and then click the **Next** button. The next Form Wizard dialog box opens, in which you choose names for the main form and the subform.

You will use Customer Orders as the main form name and Order Subform as the subform name.

4. Position the insertion point to the right of the last letter in the Form text box, press the **spacebar**, and then type **Orders**. The main form name is now Customer Orders. Note that the default subform name, Order Subform, is the name you want, so you don't need to change it.

You have answered all the Form Wizard questions.

5. Click the **Finish** button. The completed form is displayed in Form view.

Notice that some columns in the subform are not wide enough to display the field names entirely. You need to resize the columns to their best fit.

6. Double-click the pointer ╋ at the right edge of each column in the subform. The columns are resized to their best fit and all field names are fully displayed. See Figure 4-17.

Figure 4-17
Completed
form

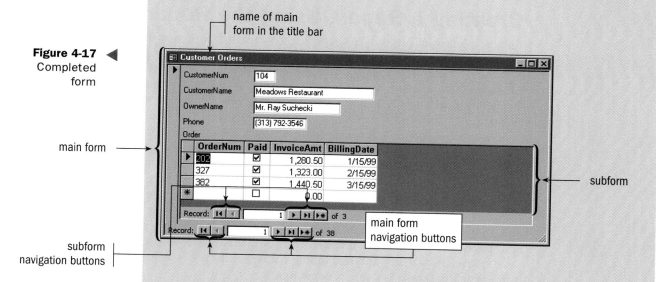

In the main form, Access displays the fields from the first record in the Customer table in columnar format. The records in the main form appear in primary key sequence by customer number. Customer 104 has three related records in the Order table; these records are shown at the bottom in a datasheet format. The form shows that Meadows Restaurant has placed three orders with Valle Coffee, and each order has been paid.

Two sets of navigation buttons appear near the bottom of the form. You use the top set of navigation buttons to select records from the related table in the subform and the bottom set to select records from the primary table in the main form.

You'll use the navigation buttons to view different records.

To navigate to different main form and subform records:

1. Click the **Last Record** navigation button ▶▎ in the main form. Record 38 in the Customer table for Embers Restaurant becomes the current record in the main form. The subform shows that this customer placed three orders with Valle Coffee, all of which are unpaid.

2. Click the **Last Record** navigation button ▶▎ in the subform. Record 3 in the Order table becomes the current record in the subform.

3. Click the **Previous Record** navigation button ◀ in the main form. Record 37 in the Customer table for The Empire becomes the current record in the main form. This customer has placed two orders, both of which are unpaid.

You have finished your work with the form, so you can close it.

4. Click the **Close** button ✕ on the form title bar. The form closes, and you return to the Database window. Notice that both the main form, Customer Orders, and the subform, Order Subform, appear in the Forms list box.

Kim would like a report showing data from both the Customer and Order tables so that all the pertinent information about restaurant customers and their orders is available in one place.

Creating a Report Using the Report Wizard

As you learned in Tutorial 1, a report is a formatted hardcopy of the contents of one or more tables in a database. In Access, you can create your own reports or use the Report Wizard to create them for you. Like the Form Wizard, the **Report Wizard** asks you a series of questions and then creates a report based on your answers. Whether you use the Report Wizard or design your own report, you can change the report's design after you create it.

Kim wants you to create a report that includes selected customer data from the Customer table and all the orders from the Order table for each customer. Kim sketched a design of the report she wants (Figure 4-18). Like the Customer Orders form you just created, which includes a main form and a subform, the report will be based on both tables, which are joined in a one-to-many relationship through the common field of CustomerNum. As shown in the sketch in Figure 4-18, the selected customer data from the primary Customer table includes the customer number, name, city, state, owner name, and phone. Below the data for each customer, the report will include the order number, paid status, invoice amount, and billing date from the related Order table. The set of field values for each order is called a **detail record**.

Figure 4-18 ◀
Report sketch
for the
Customers and
Orders report

fields from Customer
table: primary table

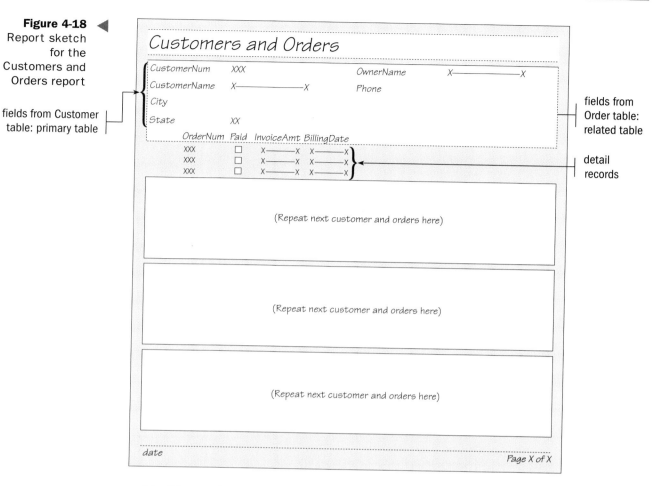

fields from
Order table:
related table

detail
records

You'll use the Report Wizard to create the report according to the design in Kim's sketch.

To activate the Report Wizard and select the fields to include in the report:

1. Click the **Reports** tab in the Database window to display the Reports list box. You have not created and saved any reports, so the list box is empty.

2. Click the **New** button in the Database window. The New Report dialog box opens.

   Although the data for the report exists in two tables (Customer and Order), you can choose only one table or query to be the data source for the report in the New Report dialog box. However, in the Report Wizard dialog boxes you can include data from other tables. You will select the primary Customer table in the New Report dialog box.

3. Click **Report Wizard**, click the list arrow for choosing a table or query, and then click **Customer**. See Figure 4-19.

Figure 4-19 ◄
Completed
New Report
dialog box

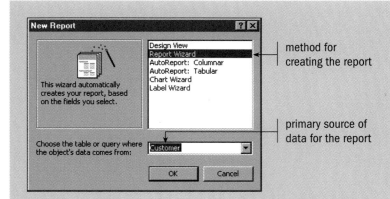

method for
creating the report

primary source of
data for the report

4. Click the **OK** button. The first Report Wizard dialog box opens.

In the first Report Wizard dialog box, you select fields in the order you want them to appear on the report. Kim wants the CustomerNum, CustomerName, City, State, OwnerName, and Phone fields from the Customer table to appear on the report.

5. Click **CustomerNum** in the Available Fields list box, and then click the [>] button. The field moves to the Selected Fields list box.

6. Repeat Step 5 for **CustomerName**, **City**, **State**, **OwnerName**, and **Phone**.

7. Click the **Tables/Queries** list arrow, and then click **Table: Order**. The fields from the Order table appear in the Available Fields list box.

The CustomerNum field will appear on the report with the customer data, so you do not have to include it in the detail records for each order. Otherwise, Kim wants all the fields from the Order table to be included in the report. The easiest way to include the necessary fields is to add all the Order table fields to the Selected Fields list box and then to remove the only field you don't want to include—CustomerNum.

8. Click the [>>] button to move all the fields from the Available Fields list box to the Selected Fields list box.

9. Click **Order.CustomerNum** in the Selected Fields list box, click the [<] button to move the selected field back to the Available Fields list box, and then click the **Next** button. The second Report Wizard dialog box opens. See Figure 4-20.

Figure 4-20 ◄
Choosing a
grouped or
ungrouped
report

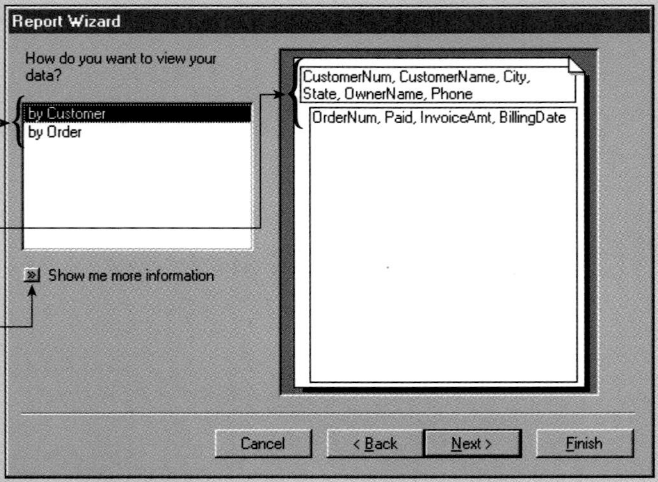

grouped by table ——

click to display
tips and examples

Report Wizard

How do you want to view your data?

by Customer
by Order

CustomerNum, CustomerName, City, State, OwnerName, Phone

OrderNum, Paid, InvoiceAmt, BillingDate

Show me more information

Cancel   < Back   Next >   Finish

You can choose to arrange the selected data grouped by table, which is the default, or ungrouped. For a grouped report, the data from a record in the primary table appears as a group, followed by the joined records from the related table. For the report you are creating, data from a record in the Customer table appears in a group, followed by the records for the customer from the Order table. An example of an ungrouped report would be a report of records from the Customer and Order tables in order by OrderNum. Each order and its associated customer data would appear together; the data would not be grouped by table.

You can display tips and examples for the choices in the Report Wizard dialog box by clicking the [>>] button ("Show me more information").

To display tips about the options in the Report Wizard dialog box:

1. Click the [>>] button. The Report Wizard Tips dialog box opens. Read the displayed information in the dialog box.

   You can display examples of different grouping methods by clicking the [>>] button ("Show me examples").

2. Click the [>>] button. The Report Wizard Examples dialog box opens. See Figure 4-21.

Figure 4-21 ◀
Report Wizard
Examples
dialog box

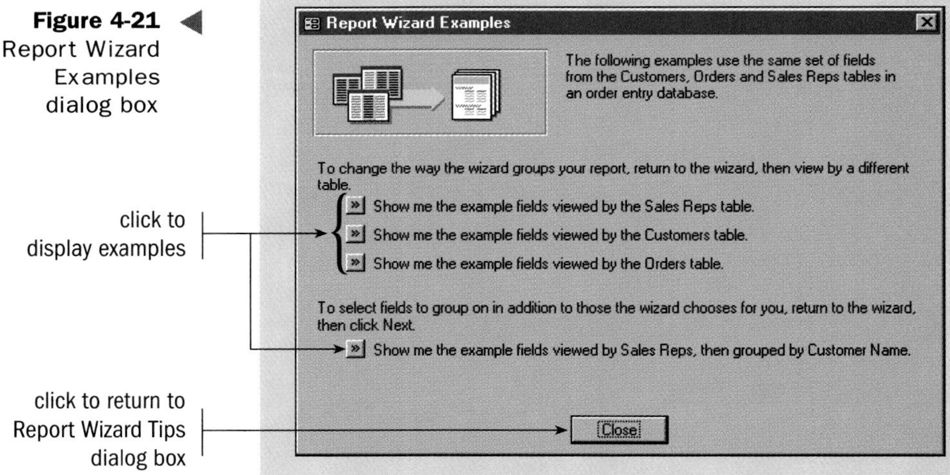

click to
display examples

click to return to
Report Wizard Tips
dialog box

You can display examples of different grouping methods by clicking the [>>] buttons.

3. Click each [>>] button in turn, review the displayed example, and then click the **Close** button to return to the Report Wizard Examples dialog box.

4. Click the **Close** button to return to the Report Wizard Tips dialog box, and then click the **Close** button to return to the second Report Wizard dialog box.

The default options shown on your screen are correct for the report Kim wants, so you can continue responding to the Report Wizard questions.

To finish creating the report using the Report Wizard:

1. Click the **Next** button. The next Report Wizard dialog box opens, in which you choose additional grouping levels.

Two grouping levels are shown: one for each customer's data, the other for a customer's orders. Grouping levels are useful for reports with multiple levels, such as those containing month, quarter, and annual totals; or containing city and country groups. Kim's report contains no further grouping levels, so you can accept the default options.

2. Click the **Next** button. The next Report Wizard dialog box opens, in which you choose the sort order for the detail records. See Figure 4-22.

Figure 4-22 ◀
Choosing the sort order for detail records

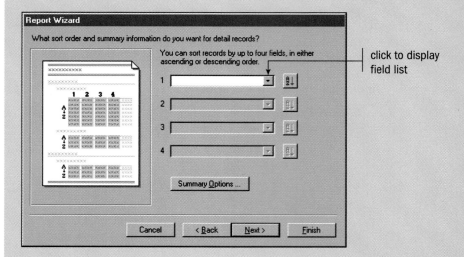

click to display field list

The records from the Order table for a customer represent the detail records for Kim's report. She wants these records to appear in increasing, or ascending, order by the value in the OrderNum field.

3. Click the **1** list arrow, click **OrderNum**, and then click the **Next** button. The next Report Wizard dialog box opens, in which you choose a layout and page orientation for the report. See Figure 4-23.

Figure 4-23 ◀
Choosing the report layout and page orientation

layout sample

orientation options

layout options

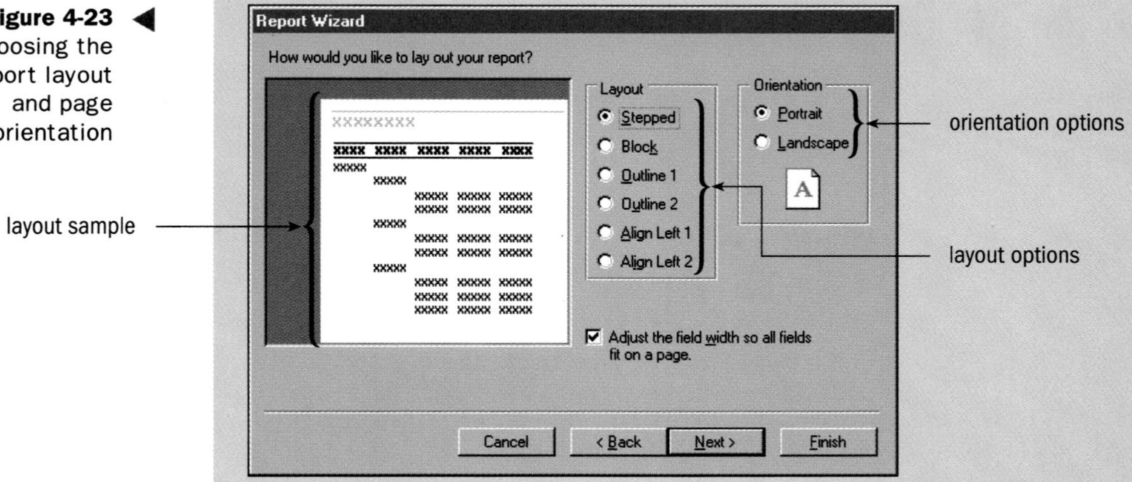

A sample of each layout appears in the box on the left.

4. Click each layout option and examine each sample that appears. You'll use the Outline 2 layout option because it resembles the layout shown in Kim's sketch of the report.

5. Click the **Outline 2** option button, and then click the **Next** button. The next Report Wizard dialog box opens, in which you choose a style for the report.

A sample of the selected style, or AutoFormat, appears in the box on the left. You can always choose a different AutoFormat after you create the report, just as you could when creating a form. Kim likes the appearance of the Corporate AutoFormat, so you'll choose this one for your report.

6. Click **Corporate** and then click the **Next** button. The last Report Wizard dialog box opens, in which you choose a report name, which also serves as the printed title on the report.

According to Kim's sketch, the report title you need to specify is "Customers and Orders."

7. Type **Customers and Orders** and then click the **Finish** button. The Report Wizard creates the report based on your answers and saves it to your Student Disk. Then Access opens the Customers and Orders report in Print Preview.

To better view the report, you need to maximize the report window.

8. Click the **Maximize** button ▢ on the Customers and Orders title bar.

To view the entire page, you need to change the Zoom setting.

9. Click the **Zoom** list arrow on the Print Preview toolbar, and then click **Fit**. The first page of the report is displayed in Print Preview. See Figure 4-24.

Figure 4-24 ◀
Report
displayed in
Print Preview

Zoom list arrow ————

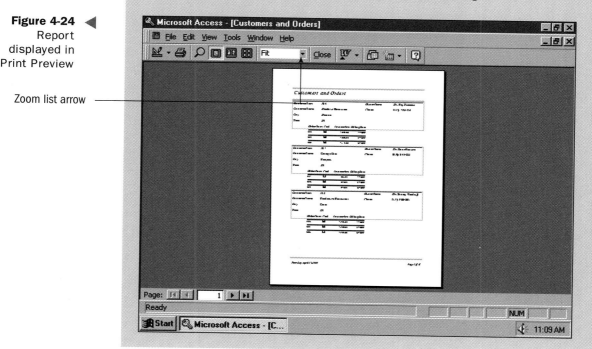

When a report is displayed in Print Preview, you can use the pointer to toggle between a full-page display and a close-up display of the report. Kim asks you to check the report to see if any adjustments need to be made. To do so, you need to view a close-up display of the report.

To view a close-up display of the report and make any necessary corrections:

1. Click the pointer ⊕ at the top center of the report. The display changes to show the report close up. See Figure 4-25.

Figure 4-25 ◀
Close-up view
of the report

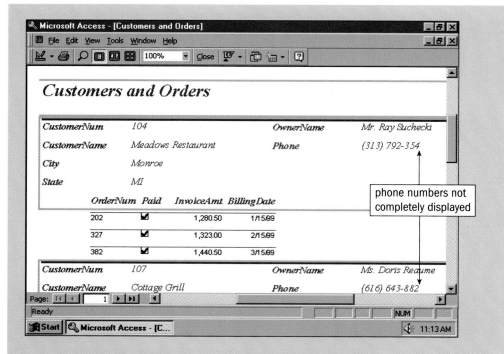

TROUBLE? Scroll your screen as necessary so that it matches the screen in Figure 4-25.

Notice that the last digit in each phone number is not visible in the report. To fix this, you need to first display the report in Design view.

2. Click the **View** button for Design view on the Print Preview toolbar. Access displays the report in Design view. See Figure 4-26.

Figure 4-26 ◀
Report
displayed in
Design view

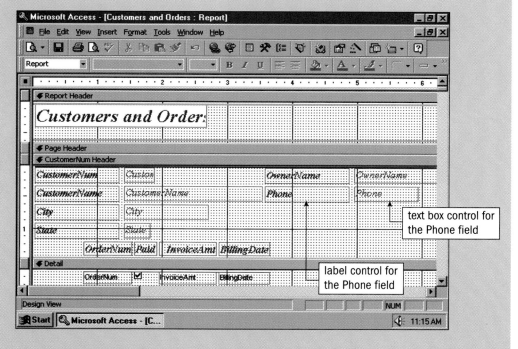

TROUBLE? If the Toolbox is displayed on your screen, close it by clicking its Close button **⊠**.

You use the Report window in Design view to modify existing reports and to create custom reports.

Each item on a report in Design view is called a *control*. For example, the Phone field consists of two controls: the label "Phone," which appears on the report to identify the field value, and the Phone text box in which the actual field value appears. You need to widen the text box control for the Phone field so that the entire field value is visible in the report.

3. Click the text box control for the Phone field to select it. Notice that small black boxes appear on the border around the control. These boxes, which are called *handles*, indicate that the control is selected and can be manipulated.

4. Position the pointer on the center right handle of the Phone text box control until the pointer changes to ↔. See Figure 4-27.

Figure 4-27 ◄
Resizing the
Phone text box
control

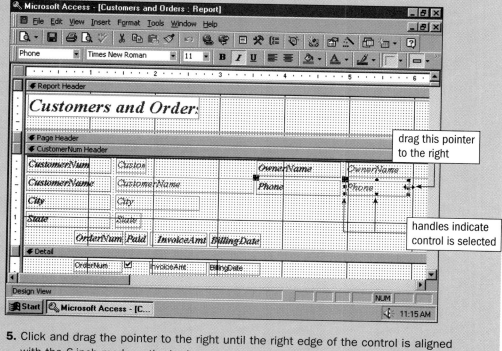

5. Click and drag the pointer to the right until the right edge of the control is aligned with the 6-inch mark on the horizontal ruler, and then release the mouse button.

Now you need to switch back to Print Preview and make sure that the complete value for the Phone field is visible.

6. Click the **View** button for Print Preview [image] on the Report Design toolbar. The report appears in Print Preview. Notice that the Phone field values are now completely displayed.

7. Click **File** on the menu bar, and then click **Save** to save the modified report.

Kim decides that she wants the report to include the Valle Coffee cup logo to the right of the report title, for visual interest. You can add the logo to the report by inserting a picture of the coffee cup.

Inserting a Picture on a Report

In Access, you can insert a picture or other graphic image on a report or form to enhance the appearance of the report or form. Sources of graphic images include Microsoft Paint, other drawing programs, and scanners. The file containing the picture you need to insert is named ValleCup, and is located in the Tutorial folder on your Student Disk.

To insert the picture on the report:

1. Click the **Close** button on the Print Preview toolbar to display the report in Design view. See Figure 4-28.

click to select Report
Header section

Figure 4-28 ◀
Inserting a
picture in
Design view

Report
Header section

insert picture here

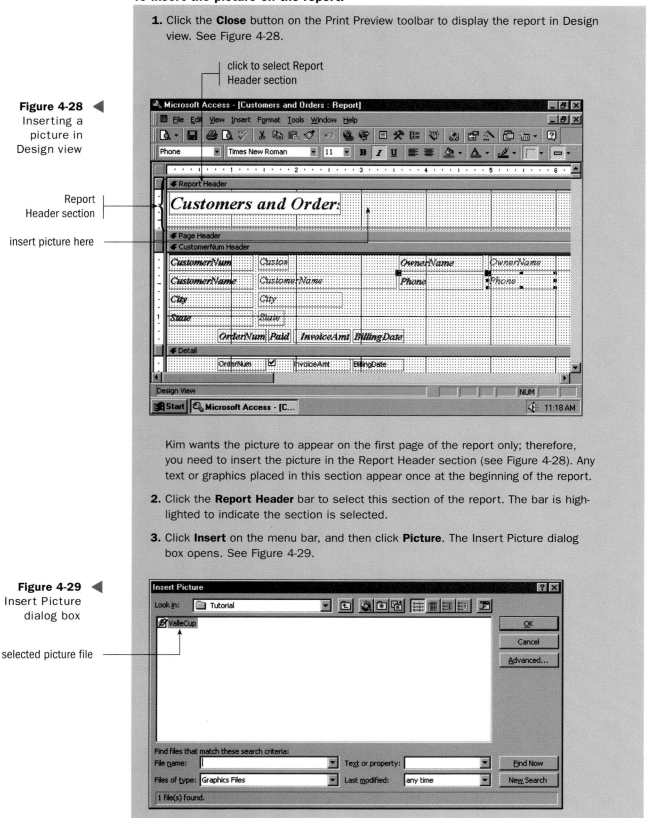

Kim wants the picture to appear on the first page of the report only; therefore, you need to insert the picture in the Report Header section (see Figure 4-28). Any text or graphics placed in this section appear once at the beginning of the report.

2. Click the **Report Header** bar to select this section of the report. The bar is highlighted to indicate the section is selected.

3. Click **Insert** on the menu bar, and then click **Picture**. The Insert Picture dialog box opens. See Figure 4-29.

Figure 4-29 ◀
Insert Picture
dialog box

selected picture file

4. Make sure Tutorial appears in the Look in text box, click **ValleCup** to select the picture of the Valle Coffee cup, and then click the **OK** button. The picture is inserted at the far left of the Report Header section, covering some of the report title text. See Figure 4-30.

Figure 4-30 ◀
Picture
inserted
in report

inserted picture ——

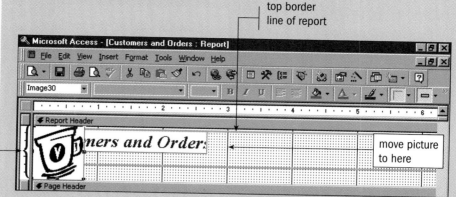

Notice that handles appear on the border around the picture, indicating that the picture is selected and can be manipulated.

Kim wants the picture to appear to the right of the report title, so you need to move the picture using the mouse.

5. Position the pointer on the picture until the pointer changes to 🖑, and then click and drag the mouse to move the picture to the right so that its left edge aligns with the 3-inch mark on the horizontal ruler and its top edge is just below the top border line above the report title (see Figure 4-30).

6. Release the mouse button. The picture appears in the new position. See Figure 4-31.

Figure 4-31 ◀
Repositioned
picture in
the report

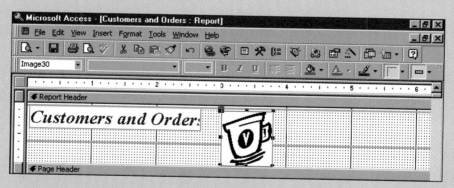

TROUBLE? If your picture is in a different location from the one shown in Figure 4-31, use the pointer 🖑 to reposition the picture until it is in approximately the same position shown in the figure. Be sure that the top edge of the picture is below the top border line of the report.

7. Click the **View** button for Print Preview 🔍 on the Report Design toolbar to view the report in Print Preview. The report now includes the inserted picture. If necessary, click the **Zoom** button 🔎 on the Print Preview toolbar to display the entire report page. See Figure 4-32.

Figure 4-32 ◀
Print Preview
of report
with picture

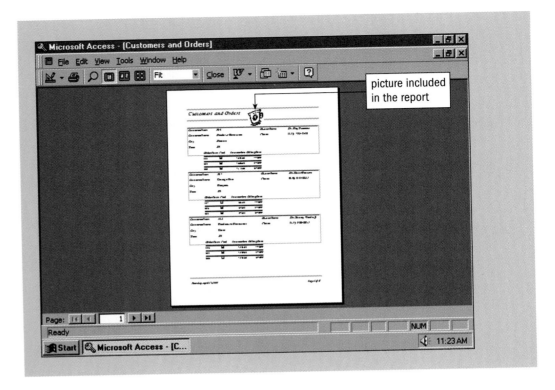

The report is now complete. You'll print a hardcopy of just the first page of the report so that Kim can review the report layout and the inserted picture.

To print page 1 of the report:

1. Click **File** on the menu bar, and then click **Print**. The Print dialog box opens.

2. In the Print Range section, click the **Pages** option button. The insertion point now appears in the From text box so that you can specify the range of pages to print.

3. Type **1** in the From text box, press the **Tab** key to move to the To text box, and then type **1**. These settings specify that only page 1 of the report will be printed.

4. Click the **OK** button. The Print dialog box closes and the first page of the report is printed. See Figure 4-33.

Access

Figure 4-33 ◀
First page
of the
Customers and
Orders report

report title

fields from
Customer table

fields from
Order table

page footer

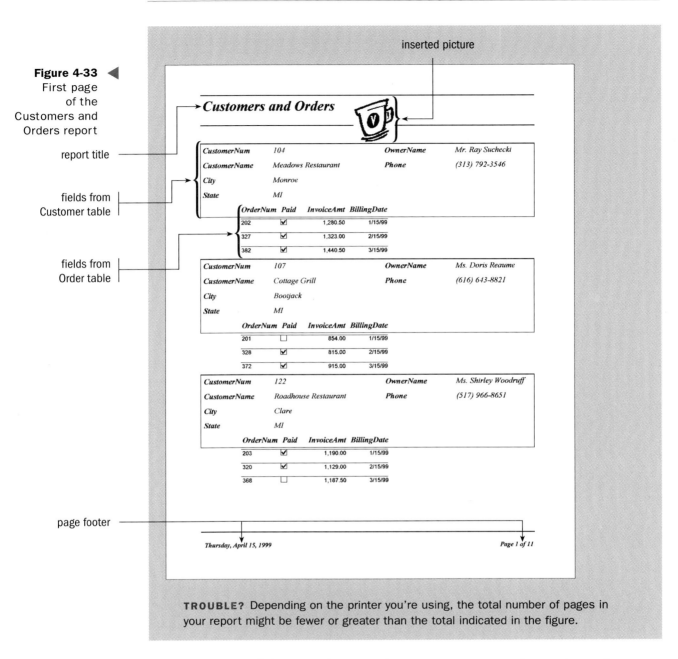

inserted picture

Customers and Orders

CustomerNum	104	OwnerName	Mr. Ray Suchecki
CustomerName	Meadows Restaurant	Phone	(313) 792-3546
City	Monroe		
State	MI		

OrderNum	Paid	InvoiceAmt	BillingDate
202	☑	1,280.50	1/15/99
327	☑	1,323.00	2/15/99
382	☑	1,440.50	3/15/99

CustomerNum	107	OwnerName	Ms. Doris Reaume
CustomerName	Cottage Grill	Phone	(616) 643-8821
City	Bootjack		
State	MI		

OrderNum	Paid	InvoiceAmt	BillingDate
201	☐	854.00	1/15/99
328	☑	815.00	2/15/99
372	☑	915.00	3/15/99

CustomerNum	122	OwnerName	Ms. Shirley Woodruff
CustomerName	Roadhouse Restaurant	Phone	(517) 966-8651
City	Clare		
State	MI		

OrderNum	Paid	InvoiceAmt	BillingDate
203	☑	1,190.00	1/15/99
320	☑	1,129.00	2/15/99
368	☐	1,187.50	3/15/99

Thursday, April 15, 1999   *Page 1 of 11*

TROUBLE? Depending on the printer you're using, the total number of pages in your report might be fewer or greater than the total indicated in the figure.

Kim approves of the report layout and contents, so you can close and save the report.

To close and save the report:

1. Click the **Close** button ☒ on the menu bar.

> **TROUBLE?** If you click the Close button on the Print Preview toolbar by mistake, Access redisplays the report in Design view. Click the Close button ☒ on the menu bar.
>
> Access displays a dialog box asking if you want to save the changes to the design of your report.

2. Click the **Yes** button to save and close the report and return to the Database window.

You no longer need to have the Database window maximized, so you can restore it now.

3. Click the **Restore** button [image] on the Database window.

Before you exit Access, you'll compact the Restaurant database to free up disk space.

Compacting a Database

When you delete records in an Access table, the space occupied by the deleted records on disk does not become available for other records. The same is true if you delete an object, such as a table, query, or form. To make the space available, you must compact the database. **Compacting** a database rearranges the data and objects in a database and creates a smaller copy of the database. Unlike making a copy of a database file, which you do to protect your database against loss or damage, you compact the database to make it smaller, thereby making more space available on your disk. Before compacting a database, you must close it.

REFERENCE window	**COMPACTING A DATABASE**
	▪ Make sure the database you want to compact is closed.
	▪ In the Access window, click Tools on the menu bar, point to Database Utilities, and then click Compact Database to open the Database to Compact From dialog box.
	▪ In the Look in box, select the drive and directory containing the database you want to compact; in the File name box, select the database you want to compact.
	▪ Click the Compact button. Access opens the Compact Database Into dialog box.
	▪ In the Save in box, select the drive and directory for the location of the compacted database; in the File name text box, type the name you want to assign to the compacted database.
	▪ Click the Save button.

You'll compact the Restaurant database, delete the original (uncompacted) database file, and then rename the compacted file.

To compact the Restaurant database:

1. Click the **Close** button [X] on the Database window title bar.

2. Click **Tools** on the menu bar, point to **Database Utilities**, and then click **Compact Database**. Access opens the Database to Compact From dialog box, in which you select the database you want to compact.

3. Make sure Tutorial appears in the Look in list box, click **Restaurant** in the list box, and then click the **Compact** button. Access opens the Compact Database Into dialog box, in which you enter the filename for the compacted copy of the database and select its drive and folder location.

Usually you would make a backup copy of the database as a safeguard before compacting. Here, you'll save the compacted database with a different name, delete the original database file, and then rename the compacted database to the original database name.

4. Type **Compacted Restaurant** in the File name text box, make sure Tutorial appears in the Look in list box, and then click the **Save** button. Access compacts the Restaurant database, creating the copied file named Compacted Restaurant, and returns you to the Access window.

Now you need to exit Access, delete the original Restaurant database, and then rename the compacted database as Restaurant. To delete and rename the necessary files, you'll open the Exploring window from the desktop.

To open the Exploring window and delete and rename the database files:

1. Click the **Close** button ⊠ on the Access window title bar. Access closes and you return to the Windows 95 desktop.

2. Using the right mouse button, click the **Start** button on the taskbar, and then click **Explore**. The Exploring window opens.

3. Scrolling as necessary, click the plus symbol to the left of the drive that contains your Student Disk in the All Folders list box, and then click **Tutorial**. The list of files in the Tutorial folder on your Student Disk appears in the Contents of 'Tutorial' list box. See Figure 4-34.

Figure 4-34
Original and compacted database files in Exploring window

original database file

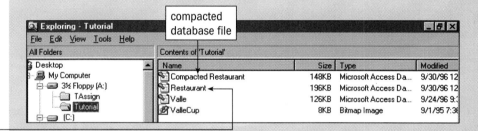

Verify that both database files—the original Restaurant database and the Compacted Restaurant database—are included in the window. Note the difference in size of the two files.

TROUBLE? The size of your files might be different from those in the figure.

Now you need to delete the original (uncompacted) database file and then rename the compacted file.

4. Click **Restaurant** in the list box, click **File** on the menu bar, and then click **Delete**. The Confirm File Delete dialog box opens and asks you to confirm the deletion.

5. Click the **Yes** button to delete the file.

6. Click **Compacted Restaurant** in the list box, click **File** on the menu bar, and then click **Rename**. The filename appears highlighted inside a box to indicate it is selected for editing.

7. Position the insertion point to the left of the word "Compacted," and then use the **Delete** key to delete the word "Compacted" and the space following it.

8. Press the **Enter** key. The filename of the compacted file is now Restaurant.

9. Click the **Close** button ⊠ on the Exploring title bar to close the Exploring window and return to the desktop.

Quick Check

1. How are a related table and a primary table associated with a form that contains a main form and a subform?

2. Describe how you use the navigation buttons to move through a form containing a main form and a subform.

3. When you use the Report Wizard, the report name is also used as the _____.

4. To insert a picture on a report, the report must be displayed in _____.

5. Any text or graphics placed in the _____ section of a report appear only on the first page of the report.

6. What is the purpose of compacting a database?

Barbara is satisfied that both forms—the Order Data form and the Customer Orders form—will make it easier to enter, view, and update data in the Restaurant database. The Customers and Orders report presents important information about Valle Coffee's restaurant customers in an attractive, professional format, which will help Kim and her staff in their sales and marketing efforts.

Tutorial Assignments

Barbara wants to enhance the Valle Products database with forms and reports, and she asks you to complete the following:

1. Make sure your Student Disk is in the disk drive, start Access, and then open the Valle Products database located in the TAssign folder on your Student Disk.

2. Use the Form Wizard to create a form based on the Product table. Select all fields for the form, the Columnar layout, the Stone style, and the title name of Product Data.

3. Using the form you created in the previous step, print the fifth form record, change the AutoFormat to Standard, save the changed form, and then print the fifth form record again.

4. Use the Product Data form to update the Product table as follows:
   a. Navigate to the record with the ProductCode 2310. Change the field values for WeightCode to A, Price to 8.99, and Decaf to Null for this record.
   b. Use the Find command to move to the record with the ProductCode 4306, and then delete the record.
   c. Add a new record with the following field values:
   ProductCode: 2306
   CoffeeCode: AMAR
   WeightCode: A
   Price: 8.99
   Decaf: Null
   Print only this form record, and then save and close the form.

5. Use the Form Wizard to create a form containing a main form and a subform. Select the CoffeeName and CoffeeType fields from the Coffee table for the main form, and select all fields except CoffeeCode from the Product table for the subform. Use the Tabular layout and the Standard style. Specify the title Coffee Products for the main form and the title Product Subform for the subform. Print the fourth main form record and its subform records.

Access

6. Use the Report Wizard to create a report based on the primary Coffee table and the related Product table. Select all fields from the Coffee table except Decaf, and select all fields from the Product table except CoffeeCode. In the third Report Wizard dialog box, specify the CoffeeType field as an additional grouping level. Sort the detail records by ProductCode. Choose the Align Left 1 layout and the Casual style for the report. Specify the title Valle Coffee Products for the report.

7. Insert the ValleCup picture, which is located in the TAssign folder on your Student Disk, in the Report Header section of the Valle Coffee Products report. Position the picture so that its left edge aligns with the 4-inch mark on the horizontal ruler and its top edge is just below the top border line of the report.

8. Print only the first page of the report, and then close and save the modified report.

9. Compact the Valle Products database; name the copy of the database Compacted Valle Products. After the compacting process is complete, delete the original Valle Products database, and then rename the Compacted Valle Products file as Valle Products.

Case Problems

1. Ashbrook Mall Information Desk Sam Bullard wants the MallJobs database to include forms and reports that will help him track and distribute information about jobs available at the Ashbrook Mall. You'll create the necessary forms and reports by completing the following:

1. Make sure your Student Disk is in the disk drive, start Access, and then open the MallJobs database located in the Cases folder on your Student Disk.

2. Use the Form Wizard to create a form based on the Store table. Select all fields for the form, the Columnar layout, and the Clouds style. Specify the title Store Data for the form.

3. Change the AutoFormat for the Store Data form to Flax.

4. Use the Find command to move to the record with the Store value of TC, and then change the Contact field value for this record to Sarah Pedicini.

5. Use the Store Data form to add a new record with the following field values:
    Store: PW
    StoreName: Pet World
    Location: B2
    Contact: Killian McElroy
    Extension: 2750
    Print only this form record, and then save and close the form.

6. Use the Form Wizard to create a form containing a main form and a subform. Select all the fields from the Store table for the main form, and select all fields except Store from the Job table for the subform. Use the Tabular layout and the Flax style. Specify the title Jobs By Store for the main form and the title Job Subform for the subform.

7. Display the Jobs By Store form in Design view. To improve the appearance of the form, you need to reduce the width of the subform so that it does not block out the Flax background. Maximize the Form window, if necessary. Click the subform to select it; handles will appear around the subform to indicate it is selected. Position the pointer on the right middle handle until the pointer changes to ↔, click and drag the mouse to the left until the right edge

of the subform aligns with the 4-inch mark on the horizontal ruler, and then release the mouse button. Restore the Form window and then display the form in Form view.

8. Print the eighth main form record and its subform records, and then save and close the Jobs By Store form.

9. Use the Report Wizard to create a report based on the primary Store table and the related Job table. Select all fields from the Store table, and select all fields from the Job table except Store. Sort the detail records by Job. Choose the Block layout and Landscape orientation for the report. Choose the Bold style. Specify the title Available Jobs for the report, and then print and close the report.

10. Compact the MallJobs database; name the copy of the database Compacted MallJobs. After the compacting process is complete, delete the original MallJobs database, and then rename the Compacted MallJobs file as MallJobs.

2. Professional Litigation User Services Raj Jawahir continues his work with the Payments database to track and analyze the payment history of PLUS clients. To help him, you'll enhance the Payments database by completing the following:

1. Make sure your Student Disk is in the disk drive, start Access, and then open the Payments database located in the Cases folder on your Student Disk.

2. Use the Form Wizard to create a form containing a main form and a subform. Select the Firm# and FirmName fields from the Firm table for the main form, and select all fields except Firm# from the Payment table for the subform. Use the Datasheet layout and the Dusk style. Specify the title Firm Payments for the main form and the title Payment Subform for the subform. Resize all columns in the subform to their best fit. Print the first main form record and its displayed subform records.

3. For the form you just created, change the AutoFormat to Colorful 2, save the changed form, and then print the first main form record and its displayed subform records.

4. Navigate to the third record in the subform for the first main record, and then change the AmtPaid field value to 1,500.00.

5. Use the Find command to move to the record with the Firm# 1136, and delete the record. Answer Yes to any warning messages about deleting the record.

6. Use the appropriate wildcard character to find all records with the abbreviation "DA" (for District Attorney) in the firm name. (*Hint:* You must enter the wildcard character before and after the text you are searching for.) How many records did you find?

7. Use the Report Wizard to create a report based on the primary Firm table and the related Payment table. Select all fields from the Firm table except Extension, and select all fields from the Payment table except Firm#. In the third Report Wizard dialog box, specify the PLUSAcctRep field as an additional grouping level. Sort the detail records by AmtPaid in *descending* order. Choose the Outline 1 layout and the Formal style for the report. Specify the title Payments By Firms for the report.

8. Insert the Plus picture, which is located in the Cases folder on your Student Disk, in the Report Header section of the Payments By Firms report. Leave the picture in its original position at the left edge of the report header.

9. Use the Office Assistant to ask the following question: "How do I move an object behind another?" Choose the topic "Move a control in front of or behind other controls." Read the information and then close the Help window. Make sure the Plus picture is still selected, and then move it behind the Payments By Firms title.

Access

10. Use the Office Assistant to ask the following question: "How do I change the background color of an object?" Choose the topic "Change the background color of a control or section." Read the information and then close the Help window and the Office Assistant. Select the Payments By Firms title object, and then change its background color to Transparent. Select each of the two horizontal lines in the Report Header section that cut through the middle of the Plus picture, and then use the Delete key to delete each line.

11. Display the report in Print Preview. Print just the first page of the report, and then close and save the report.

12. Compact the Payments database; name the copy of the database Compacted Payments. After the compacting process is complete, delete the original Payments database, and then rename the Compacted Payments file as Payments.

3. Best Friends Noah and Sheila Warnick want to create forms and reports for the Walks database. You'll help them create these database objects by completing the following:

1. Make sure your Student Disk is in the disk drive, start Access, and then open the Walks database located in the Cases folder on your Student Disk.

2. Use the Form Wizard to create a form based on the Walker table. Select all fields for the form, the Columnar layout, and the Colorful 1 style. Specify the title Walker Data for the form.

3. Use the Walker Data form to update the Walker table as follows:
   a. For the record with the WalkerID 223, change the LastName to Hoban and the Distance to 0.
   b. Add a new record with the following values:
      WalkerID: 225
      LastName: DelFavero
      FirstName: Cindi
      Phone: 711-1275
      Distance: 2.0
      Print just this form record.
   c. Delete the record with the WalkerID field value of 123.

4. Change the AutoFormat of the Walker Data form to Pattern, save the changed form, and then use the form to print the last record in the Walker table. Close the form.

5. Use the Form Wizard to create a form containing a main form and a subform. Select all the fields from the Walker table for the main form, and select the PledgeAmt, PaidAmt, and DatePaid fields from the Pledge table for the subform. Use the Tabular layout and the Standard style. Specify the title Walkers And Pledges for the main form and the title Pledge Subform for the subform. Use the navigation buttons to find the first main form record that contains values in the subform. Print this main form record and its subform records.

6. Use the Report Wizard to create a report based on the primary Walker table and the related Pledge table. Select all fields from the Walker table, and select all fields from the Pledge table except WalkerID. Sort the detail records by PledgeNo. Choose the Align Left 2 layout and Landscape orientation for the report. Choose the Soft Gray style. Specify the title Walk-A-Thon Walkers And Pledges for the report.

7. View both pages of the report in Print Preview. (*Hint:* Use a toolbar button.) Notice that the pledge data for the third record appears at the top of the second page. You need to decrease the size of the bottom margin so that the pledge data will appear with its corresponding walker data. Use the Office Assistant to ask the question, "How do I change the margins in a report?" Choose the topic "Set margins, page orientation, and other page setup options" and then read the displayed Help information. Use the Page Setup command to change the bottom margin of the report to .5".

8. Print the entire report.

9. Compact the Walks database; name the copy of the database "Compacted Walks." After the compacting process is complete, delete the original Walks database, and then rename the Compacted Walks file as Walks.

4. Lopez Lexus Dealerships Maria and Hector Lopez want to create forms and reports that will help them track and analyze data about the cars and different locations for their Lexus dealerships. Help them enhance the Lexus database by completing the following:

1. Make sure your Student Disk is in the disk drive, start Access, and then open the Lexus database located in the Cases folder on your Student Disk.

2. Use the Form Wizard to create a form containing a main form and a subform. Select all the fields from the Locations table for the main form, and select the VehicleID, Model, Class, Year, Cost, and SellingPrice fields from the Cars table for the subform. Use the Datasheet layout and the International style. Specify the title Locations And Cars for the main form and the title Cars Subform for the subform. Resize all columns in the subform to their best fit. Print the first main form record and its displayed subform records.

3. For the form you just created, change the AutoFormat to Standard, save the changed form, and then print the first main form record and its displayed subform records.

4. Navigate to the second record in the subform for the fifth main record, and then change the SellingPrice field value to $42,175.00.

5. Use the Find command to move to the record with the LocationCode P1, and delete the record. Answer Yes to any warning messages about deleting the record.

6. Use the appropriate wildcard character to find all records with a LocationCode value that begins with the letter "A." How many records did you find?

7. Use the Report Wizard to create a report based on the primary Locations table and the related Cars table. Select all fields from the Locations table, and select all fields from the Cars table except Manufacturer and LocationCode. Specify two sort fields for the detail records: first, the VehicleID field in ascending order, then the Cost field in descending order. Choose the Align Left 1 layout and Landscape orientation for the report. Choose the Compact style. Specify the title Dealership Locations And Cars for the report, and then print just the first page of the report.

8. Compact the Lexus database; name the copy of the database Compacted Lexus. After the compacting process is complete, delete the original Lexus database, and then rename the Compacted Lexus file as Lexus.

Answers to Quick Check Questions

SESSION 1.1

1 field

2 common field

3 primary key; foreign key

4 records; fields

5 current record symbol

6 Use the horizontal and vertical scroll bars to view fields or records not currently visible in the datasheet; use the navigation buttons to move vertically through the records.

SESSION 1.2

1 query

2 primary key

3 AutoForm Wizard

4 The form displays each field name on a separate line to the left of its field value, which appears in a box; the widths of the boxes represent the size of the fields.

5 Click the Office Assistant button on any toolbar, type a question in the text box, click the Search button, and then choose a topic from the list displayed.

6 Print Preview

SESSION 2.1

1 Identify all the fields needed to produce the required information; group related fields into tables; determine each table's primary key; include a common field in related tables; avoid data redundancy; and determine the properties of each field.

2 The data type determines what field values you can enter for the field and what other properties the field will have.

3 text fields and number fields

4 Order numbers will not be used for calculations.

5 null

6 the record being edited; the next row available for a new record

SESSION 2.2

1 The field and all its values are removed from the table.

2 In Design view, right-click the row selector for the row above which you want to insert the field, click Insert Rows on the shortcut menu, and then define the new field.

3 yes/no

4 Format property

5 Access allows you to have only one database open at a time.

6 In navigation mode, the entire field value is selected and anything you type replaces the field value; in editing mode, you can insert or delete characters in a field value based on the location of the insertion point.

SESSION 3.1

1 a general query in which you specify the fields and records you want Access to select

2 The field list contains the table name at the top of the list box and the table's fields listed in the order in which they appear in the table; the design grid displays columns that contain specifications about a field you will use in the query.

3 A table datasheet and a query datasheet look the same, appearing in Datasheet view, and can be used to update data in a database. A table datasheet shows the permanent data in a table, whereas a query datasheet is temporary and its contents are based on the criteria you establish in the design grid.

4 primary table; related table

5 referential integrity

6 oldest to most recent date

7 when you have two or more nonadjacent sort keys or when the fields to be used for sorting are in the wrong order

8 filter

SESSION 3.2

1 condition

2 in the same Criteria row; in different Criteria rows

3 expression

4 A calculated field appears in a query datasheet but does not exist in a database, as does a table field.

5 a function that performs an arithmetic operation on selected records in a database

6 Group By

SESSION 4.1

1 The AutoForm Wizard creates a form automatically using all the fields in the selected table or query; the Form Wizard allows you to choose some or all of the fields in the selected table or query, choose fields from other tables and queries, and display fields in any order on the form.

2 An AutoFormat is a predefined style for a form (or report). To change a form's AutoFormat, display the form in Design view, click the AutoFormat button on the Form Design toolbar, click the new AutoFormat in the Form AutoFormats list box, and then click OK.

3 the last record in the table

4 datasheet

5 the question mark (?)

6 as many form records as can fit on a printed page

7 Click the record selector in the top left of the form.

SESSION 4.2

1 The main form displays the data from the primary table and the subform displays the data from the related table.

2 You use the top set of navigation buttons to select and move through records from the related table in the subform and the bottom set to select and move through records from the primary table in the main form.

3 report title

4 Design view

5 Report Header

6 to make the database smaller and make more space available on your disk

Microsoft Access 97 **Index**

Special Characters
  ! (exclamation point), A 4.8
  # (number sign), A 4.8
  * (asterisk), A 4.8, A 4.9
  - (hyphen), A 4.8
  ? (question mark), A 4.8
  [] (square brackets), A 4.8

A Access, A 1.3
    exiting, A 1.13, A 1.22, A 2.27
    Help system, A 1.18–1.20
    starting, A 1.7–1.9
  Access window, A 1.10
  aggregate functions, A 3.31–3.33
    grouped, A 3.33–3.34
  And logical operator, A 3.24, A 3.25
  asterisk (*), wildcard character, A 4.8,
    A 4.9
  AutoFormat dialog box, A 4.5
  AutoFormats, A 4.4–4.6
  AutoForm Wizard, A 1.16–1.17
  AutoNumber data type, A 2.5
  AutoReport: Columnar Wizard,
    A 1.21–1.22
  Avg function, A 3.31

B brackets ([]), wildcard character, A 4.8

C calculated fields, A 3.28–3.31
    adding to queries, A 3.29–3.31
  calculations, A 3.28–3.34
    aggregate functions, A 3.31–3.33
    calculated fields, A 3.28–3.31
    groups of records, A 3.33–3.34

cascade deletes option, A 3.8
cascade updates option, A 3.8
changing. *See* modifying; modifying table
  structure
closing
    forms, A 1.16
    Office Assistant, A 1.9
    reports, A 1.22, A 4.27
column selectors, A 1.11
column width, datasheets, A 3.22
common fields, A 1.5–1.6
    designing databases, A 2.3
compacting databases, A 4.28–4.29
comparison operators, A 3.18–3.19
    matching ranges of values, A 3.23–3.24
composite keys, A 2.2–2.3
conditions, A 3.18. *See also* selection criteria
controls, size, A 4.23
copying records from another Access data-
    base, A 2.22–2.24
Count function, A 3.31
Currency data type, A 2.5
current record symbol, A 1.12

D data, organizing, A 1.5
  database management systems (DBMSs),
    A 1.6–1.7
  databases, A 1.5–1.6, A 2.1–2.27
    compacting, A 4.28–4.29
    deleting, A 4.29
    designing, A 2.2–2.3
    opening, A 1.9–1.10, A 2.6
    querying. *See* queries
    renaming, A 4.29
    saving, A 2.16–2.17
    tables. *See* modifying table structure;
      tables; table structure
    updating. *See* updating databases

Microsoft Access 97 **Task Reference**

TASK	PAGE #	RECOMMENDED METHOD
Access, exit	A 1.13	Click ☒ on the program window
Access, start	A 1.7	Click Start, point to Programs, click Microsoft Access
Aggregate functions, use	A 3.31	Display the query in Design view, click Σ
AutoForm, create	A 1.16	Click the Forms tab, click New, click an AutoForm Wizard, choose the table or query for the form, click OK
AutoFormat, change	A 4.4	See Reference Window: Changing a Form's AutoFormat
AutoReport, create	A 1.21	Click the Reports tab, click New, click an AutoReport Wizard, choose the table or query for the form, click OK
Calculated field, add to a query	A 3.28	See Reference Window: Using Expression Builder
Column, adjust width of	A 3.21	Double-click the right border of the column heading
Data, find	A 4.7	See Reference Window: Finding Data
Database, compact	A 4.28	See Reference Window: Compacting a Database
Datasheet view, switch to	A 2.14	Click ▦
Design view, switch to	A 2.18	Click ⩗
Field, add	A 2.19	See Reference Window: Adding a Field Between Two Existing Fields
Field, define	A 2.8	See Reference Window: Defining a Field in a Table
Field, delete	A 2.18	Display the table in Design view, right-click the field's row selector, click Delete Rows
Field, move	A 2.19	Display the table in Design view, click the field's row selector, drag the field with the pointer
Filter By Selection, activate	A 3.16	Select the field value, click ⧩
Form Wizard, activate	A 4.2	Click the Forms tab, click New, click Form Wizard, choose the table or query for the form, click OK
Office Assistant, use to get Help	A 1.18	See Reference Window: Using the Office Assistant
Picture, insert on a report	A 4.24	Click Insert on the menu bar, click Picture, select the picture file, click OK
Primary key, specify	A 2.12	See Reference Window: Specifying a Primary Key for a Table
Query, define	A 3.3	Click the Queries tab, click New, click Design View, click OK
Query, run	A 3.5	Click ❗
Query results, sort	A 3.14	See Reference Window: Sorting a Query Datasheet

Microsoft Access 97 **Task Reference**

TASK	PAGE #	RECOMMENDED METHOD
Record, add a new one	A 1.12	Click [▶*]
Record, delete	A 2.25	Right-click the record's row selector, click Delete Record, click Yes
Record, move to first	A 1.12	Click [◄◄]
Record, move to last	A 1.12	Click [►►]
Record, move to next	A 1.12	Click [►]
Record, move to previous	A 1.12	Click [◄]
Record, move to a specific one	A 1.12	Type the record number in the Specific Record box, press Enter
Records, redisplay all after filter	A 3.17	Click [▼]
Relationship, define between two tables	A 3.8	Click [⊟]
Report Wizard, activate	A 4.17	Click the Reports tab, click New, click Report Wizard, choose the table or query for the report, click OK
Sort, specify ascending	A 3.12	Click [A↓]
Sort, specify descending	A 3.12	Click [Z↓]
Table, create	A 2.6	Click the Tables tab, click New, click Design View, click OK
Table, open	A 1.11	Click the Tables tab, click the table name, click Open
Table, print	A 1.13	Click [🖨]
Table structure, save	A 2.13	See Reference Window: Saving a Table Structure